TEN LIVES OF THE
Buddha

Ten Lives of the
Buddha
Siamese Temple Painting and Jataka Tales

by Elizabeth Wray, Clare Rosenfield,
and Dorothy Bailey
with photographs by Joe D. Wray

New York • Weatherhill • Tokyo

First edition, 1972
Revised paperback edition, 1996

Published by Weatherhill, Inc., of New York and Tokyo, with editorial offices at 568 Broadway, Suite 705, New York, N.Y. 10012.

Library of Congress Cataloging-in-Publication Data

Wray, Elizabeth.
  Ten Lives of the Buddha : Siamese temple paintings and Jataka tales / by
Elizabeth Wray, Clare Rosenfield, and Dorothy Bailey ; with photographs
by Joe D. Wray. — Rev. ed.
       p.   cm.
  Originally published: New York : Weatherhill, 1972.
  Includes bibliographical references.
  ISBN 0-8348-0374-7 (pbk.)
    1. Tipiṭaka. Suttapiṭaka. Khuddakanikāya. Jātaka—Criticism, interpretation, etc.
2. Tipiṭaka. Suttapiṭaka. Khuddakanikāya. Jātaka—Illustrations.   3. Mural
painting and decoration, Thai.   4. Gautama Buddha—Pre-existence.
I. Rosenfield, Clare.   II. Bailey, Dorothy.   III. Wray, Joe D.   IV. Tipiṭaka.
Suttapiṭaka. Khuddakanikāya. Jātaka. English. Selections.   V. Title.
BQ1467.W43   1996
294.3'823—dc20
                                                              96-9424
                                                              CIP

Dedicated with gratitude to
VICTOR KENNEDY
who introduced us to the fascinating world
of Thai art and assisted in our pursuit
of the Jatakas in Thai mural painting

CONTENTS AND ILLUSTRATIONS

FOREWORD

THE BEAUTY of Siamese religious painting is not intended to please the eye as an end in itself but to enlist people's attention in order to tell them a story. The wall paintings discussed in this book illustrate the ten most important Jataka tales, stories of the Buddha's previous lives in which he was still a *bodhisatta* striving to accumulate a sufficient store of merit and wisdom to be able to achieve Buddhahood by a supreme effort in his final life. Everything in these pictures means something; nothing is merely decorative. If flowers are seen falling from heaven, they are not there simply to fill a space, they are being thrown down by the gods to celebrate a miracle; the jeweled attire of gods and princes denotes the happy state resulting from merits they have made in past lives; architecture, landscape, and genre scenes specify the type of place in which the action occurs.

Dr. Wray's photographs, besides introducing the general reader to an art which will very likely be new to him, will be a great help to specialists, even those who live in Bangkok. Studying Siamese wall painting *in situ* requires both patience and agility. Many things about them can be studied better by comparing one photograph with another than by running from monastery to monastery, looking for the man who has the key to the building that contains the murals, and climbing a ladder to examine the dimly lighted portions near the ceiling. No matter how well a person may know the paintings, Dr. Wray's photographs are likely to show him some details that have escaped him.

In a sense these paintings—like all pictures designed to illustrate specific texts—have no independent existence. It is true that we can learn a great deal about Siamese architecture, warfare, dress, manners, customs, court life, and the daily life of the people in the eighteenth and nineteenth centuries from them, for the ancient Indian tales are transposed into a Siamese setting of the painter's own day, or sometimes a setting inspired in part by slightly older Siamese paintings of the same subject: the happy anachronism serves as a reminder that the lessons the tales teach are timeless. Apart from such incidental benefits, however, it would not be very satisfying to study the illustrations of texts without knowing the content of the texts themselves; and for this information the reader has only to turn the pages to the elegant exposition offered by Mrs. Wray, Mrs. Rosenfield, and Mrs. Bailey. The authors review the plots of the ten Jatakas illustrated; they give a brief history of the Jataka collection; they tell us something about the development of Jataka illustrations in the arts of India, Ceylon, and Southeast Asia, with the chief emphasis on Burma and Siam; and they provide a chapter on Siamese temple painting which, among much other useful information, will help the reader to understand the conventions of an art which might otherwise be puzzling.

Siamese wall paintings have received surprisingly little attention in the West. Not counting pamphlets, this is the first book on the subject with photographs taken directly from the originals. The photographs in *The Life of the Buddha According to Thai Temple Paintings*, issued by the United States Information Service in Bangkok on the occasion of the year 2500 of the Buddhist Era (A.D. 1957), are taken not from the murals themselves, many of which are badly defaced, but from copies of them painted by R. W. E. Hampe, in which—as befits a publication for a religious occasion—the artist has repaired the losses. Indeed, not many photographs of Siamese murals have been published at all. A few have appeared in travel books, a few in articles in Bangkok magazines which have all too brief a life expectancy, a few in the *Journal of the Siam Society*, a few in pamphlets issued by the Department of Fine Arts in Bangkok. The most informative of these pamphlets are by Miss Elizabeth Lyons, who has devoted years of study to the subject. Miss Lyons promises us a book on Siamese traditional painting in all its forms, which will probably appear this year. The three books *The Life of the Buddha* with Mr. Hampe's pictures, the present volume, and Miss Lyons' forthcoming work, all serving different purposes, should supplement one another nicely.

In *Ten Lives of the Buddha* we have a richly varied sample of Siamese Jataka paintings, many of them never published before, and a text which cannot fail to heighten the reader's appreciation of them. To anyone who already knows these paintings, which illustrate tales that have exerted an enduring influence on Siamese life, the book will be a delight. To anyone who does not know them it will be a revelation.

A. B. GRISWOLD

AUTHORS' PREFACE

IN AUGUST, 1967, a group of fifteen American women living in Bangkok began meeting weekly to study the meaning and forms of Thai art. They were fortunate in finding Victor Kennedy, a young Australian teacher who had lived in Thailand for over eight years, to instruct them. He had traveled extensively in Thailand, visited scores of Buddhist monasteries and historic sites, read widely in the field of Asian art and culture, and written articles for the local press. Under his tutelage, members of the Thai History Study Group became acquainted with the art of the Bangkok-Thonburi-Ayuthaya area. They focused on certain topics: mythical animals, Thai architecture, Thai painting, and Jataka tales.

In March, 1968, it was suggested that the remaining members of the study group undertake to rewrite the ten Jataka tales most popular in Thailand and illustrate them with photographs of temple paintings depicting the tales. Five members were interested in the project and launched into it with gusto. Unfortunately, two of them, Sara Hutchinson and Nena Shepherd, had to leave Thailand later that year; the present three authors continued to work on the manuscript, while Joe Wray agreed to photograph the murals.

All three authors collaborated on adapting the stories. As the book evolved, it became apparent that some explanatory material was required. Dorothy Bailey worked on the Introduction, while Clare Rosenfield and Elizabeth Wray devoted their time to the essays on the Jataka tales and Siamese temple painting. However, each author edited and contributed to the others' work, so that the final version represents the combined effort of three minds and three pens.

The authors were helped by a number of kind friends. Primary credit for the existence of the book is due Mr. Victor Kennedy, who assisted in the initial stages and helped us acquire much of the background for the present volume. We are grateful to Dr. Scott Elledge, Professor of English, Cornell University; Dr. Theodore Bowie, Professor of Oriental Art, Indiana University; and Dr. John Rosenfield, Professor of Buddhist Art, Harvard University, who read the manuscript at various stages and offered useful comments. Particular thanks are due to Mr. A. B. Griswold, Visiting Professor at Cornell University, and one of the foremost authorities on the art of Thailand, for his pertinent suggestions and careful criticism.

We also appreciate very much the help of Mr. Hiram Woodward, Jr., of Yale University, who gave so generously of his time in scrutinizing the text with care and answering many of our questions.

To His Highness Prince Dhani Nivat, Kromamun Bidayalabh Brdihyakorn; Dr. David Casey, and Mr. Roger Welty, who contributed to our understanding of Buddhism, we owe a special word of thanks.

We should like to express our gratitude to Mrs. Bonnie Crown of the Asia Society, New York, who provided encouragement when it was most needed.

To Khun Choosak Dipayagasorn, head of the Manuscripts and Inscriptions Section of the Department of Fine Arts, and Khun Pitoon Malwan, assistant head of the Art and Literature Section, we also convey our thanks for their help in tracing the Jatakas in Siam.

Our appreciation is due to three friends who typed the manuscript for us, Chongchitt Resanondhi, Papit Gualtieri, and Margaret Thomlinson, and to Jenny Piastunovich for her editorial comments.

Most of all, we wish to thank our patient husbands, Joe D. Wray, Allan G. Rosenfield, and Gordon B. Bailey, who encouraged us and bore with us. To Joe Wray, who cheerfully devoted many weekends to photographing the murals and many hours to preparing the maps and diagram, we are especially grateful.

With regard to the language and spelling used, it should be noted that in the translation of the Jataka from Pali into English on which these ten stories are based, the Pali terms of Theravada Buddhism are used. We have adhered to the Pali vocabulary except when referring to Mahayana Buddhism, where Sanskrit terms are more appropriate. Thus, except in specific reference to Mahayana Buddhism, the Pali word *Bodhisatta* is used instead of the Sanskrit *Bodhisattva*, and Pali *Nibbana* rather than Sanskrit *Nirvana*. Both forms of such Buddhist terms are included in the Glossary.

In spelling names of cities and monasteries in Thailand, we have adhered to the phonetic system developed by the Royal Institute of Thailand, except that diacritical marks have been omitted in the body of the book. These marks are supplied in the List of Alternate Spellings at the back of the book, together with the spellings of these names in accordance with the graphic system. The graphic system, which transliterates names from Sanskrit or Pali according to their spelling in the original language rather than phonetically, is also in wide use and has the advantage of showing the linguistic derivation of the names more clearly than the phonetic system. The meanings of the names are also included in the list.

INTRODUCTION

FOR CENTURIES, mural paintings have illuminated the walls of Buddhist temples in Siam. In gay and vivid style, they depict a variety of scenes whose meaning is obscure to the uninitiated. Usually the scenes are from two of the themes most popular in Buddhist art from its beginnings: the life of the Buddha and tales of his previous incarnations, called Jatakas.

Many of these tales are of great antiquity, having their origins in a body of fables and legends which date from ancient, pre-Buddhist days in India. From time immemorial, such parables and heroic stories were told by one generation to the next, often in verse form. As these were part of the common folklore of India, it is likely that when the Buddha taught in the sixth century B.C. he was familiar with the tales and illustrated his sermons with them. After the Buddha's death, his teachings, inscribed in the minds of his disciples, were recited often and thus preserved. Certain monks called *bhanakas* memorized different passages of the doctrine, or Dhamma, so that the Buddha's discourses were faithfully remembered and eventually became the Buddhist scriptures.

By the second century B.C., the tales had become known by the name Jataka, or birth story. According to Buddhist history, they were first written down in the first century B.C. in Ceylon along with the rest of the Buddhist scriptures and their commentaries, but these manuscripts no longer exist. The oldest extant version of the scriptures dates to the fifth century A.D. and is written in Pali, the language of Theravada Buddhism, which is practiced in Ceylon and much of Southeast Asia. The fifth-century compilation of 547 Jataka tales was translated from Pali into English by the Pali Text Society of London in 1906 under the title *The Jataka*.

The final ten stories of this collection have been accorded a special place of honor by Buddhists through the centuries. In Pali they are called *Dasajati* (Ten Births, or Ten Lives); they have the same name in Siam, though pronounced *Thotsachat*. However, the Thais more frequently call them *Phra Chao Sip Chat* (Ten Lives of Our Lord).

In the Jatakas the central character, whether animal, human, or semidivine, is a Bodhisatta, or Buddha-to-be. Although in some of the stories he is only a passive onlooker, in most of the tales he practices one or more of the ten virtues which must be perfected in order to become a Buddha. In the final ten tales, the culmination of countless lives leading toward Buddhahood

—of which 547 are only a fraction—all ten virtues are brought to perfection. Each story depicts one of the virtues: the story of Temiya exemplifies the virtue of renunciation; Mahajanaka, courage; Sama, lovingkindness; Nimi, resolution; Mahosadha, wisdom; Bhuridatta, perseverance; Canda-Kumara, forbearance; Narada, equanimity; Vidhura-Pandita, truthfulness; and Vessantara, charity. The stories are still taught to Thai schoolchildren as models of good conduct. Buddhist monks sometimes read them as sermons, and in many Thai *wats,* or monasteries, especially in the north, the Vessantara story is retold each year at an annual festival called *Thet Mahachat,* or Sermon of the Great Birth Story.

Ever since Buddhist monuments have been built, scenes from the Jatakas have been used to decorate them. They have been the subject of sculpture and painting throughout Buddhist Asia. These illustrations are not merely ornamental; their primary function is to teach. In Siam, the last ten tales are seen much more often than the other Jatakas. Cloth banners, lacquerware cabinets, manuscripts, and temple walls all reflect the affection felt by Thai Buddhists for these stories. Unfortunately, a history of repeated Burmese invasions, adverse weather conditions, impermanent painting techniques, and an acceptance of the natural deterioration of all things have contributed to the loss of much Thai mural painting. However, there remain more than a dozen wats scattered in the towns and countryside of Siam in which murals of the last ten Jatakas, painted in a style characteristic of traditional Thai art, may be found.

In order to make sense of the wall paintings, where each story is told through a small number of representative scenes, one must be familiar with the tales. The translation of the 547 stories by the Pali Text Society fills six volumes in which the stories are arranged, as in the Pali text, in order of length beginning with the shortest. The final volume is devoted entirely to the last ten. As they are long and full of detail, we thought that a brief retelling of these ten tales might be welcome.

In our version, each story is related as it is portrayed in Thai murals. We have omitted certain episodes of the Pali text which are not usually depicted in these paintings. The tales are told from the viewpoint of one looking at the scenes most commonly chosen by Thai painters to convey the narrative.

It is not known if the muralists were acquainted with the Pali scriptural version. They may have relied on Thai translations, which were somewhat different from the fifth-century Pali text. It is also possible that the abbot, or some other learned monk from the monastery, chose and described the scenes he wished the artist to paint.

Portrayed in the murals is a fairy-tale world, inhabited by mythical creatures, divinities, and human beings of all sorts. However, from the written text of the stories, it is possible to visualize what life was like in India at the time the Buddha lived and during the next several centuries. The setting of the Jataka tales was the broad Gangetic plain of northeast India. To the north rose the peaks of the Himalayas; in the south was the lower Vindhya range. The fertile plain was well watered by the Ganges and its tributaries. The people lived in market towns and villages, with most of the population engaged in farming and cattle raising. Often of the same clan, the villagers shared common rights over pasture and forest land. Artisans who worked in guilds wandered from town to town or occupied villages of their own.

Separating the settlements were remnants of the great forest which must have once covered almost the entire plain. Always on the periphery of the people's lives, the forest provided a convenient refuge for robbers or runaway slaves and a retreat for those who wished to escape from the burdens of everyday existence to a life of solitude.

Politically, the great plain was divided among several large kingdoms and a number of smaller ones. Each kingdom was ruled from a capital city, a citadel surrounded by a moat encircling the wall or embankment which protected the city. It served as a fortress and was also a center of trade and entertainment for villagers from the surrounding region and for passing travelers.

The spread of Vedic culture in northern India, beginning with the arrival of the first Aryans around 1700 B.C. and continuing into the first millennium, brought common social institutions and religion. The religion was called Brahmanism, a combination of the beliefs of the earlier inhabitants of India, the Dravidians, and ideas introduced by the Aryan invaders. Brahmanic gods were the personifications of great natural forces: among these deities were Indra, god of thunder; Agni, god of fire; and Surya, god of the sun. Brahman was the universal spirit; Brahma, the creator.

According to Brahmanic doctrine, men were divided into various classes that sprang from Brahma. From his mouth came the Brahmins, or priests, from his arms the Kshatriyas, or warriors. The Vaisyas, cultivators and traders, sprang from his thighs, and from his feet came the Sudras, or serfs. Originally devised to maintain the purity of the Aryan peoples, who constituted the first three classes, as distinguished from the dark-skinned Dravidians, who were the Sudras, these classes eventually proliferated into hundreds of castes.

The kings were drawn from the Kshatriya, or warrior, class. Each king was a focal point in the social organization. He was thought to possess special virtues and was expected to be an example to his subjects as well as responsible for their conduct. All the business of the state, including the administration of justice, was under his jurisdiction.

Vying for equal, if not greater, status were the Brahmins, so often seen in the Jatakas. The kings often depended for advice upon Brahmin priests, who were considered to be repositories of knowledge. The Brahmins also held great powers through their officiation at the sacrifices necessary to insure the goodwill of the Brahmanic gods.

Over the centuries, the lives of the people became more and more tightly bound in ritual. Every new undertaking, every important occasion required the presence of a priest. Without the proper ceremony and special words, the outcome could not be auspicious. However, as the Brahmin class grew too numerous for all to earn their living as priests, many entered various trades. Not all were worthy of respect, for, as with all men, there were some who were not only foolish but wicked.

Along with the rites of Brahmanism existed another form of religious expression. From ancient times in India there had been wandering mendicants or sages who renounced worldly concerns and withdrew to the life of asceticism. Some practiced various disciplines of meditation in an effort to attain spiritual exaltation. Others went to great extremes of austerity and self-torture in order to achieve *tapas*, meaning a burning glow and signifying a state of mental bliss. Starvation was only a minor form of the suffering they endured, often living in caves in the woods and eating only the nuts and berries the forest provided. There seems to have been no idea of penance attached to these disciplines, however. Ascetic practices were a sign of moral superiority, of man's indifference to pain, and were performed with the purpose of achieving heightened spiritual powers.

Many of the ideas of Brahmanism were carried into the Buddhist religion, such as a belief in reincarnation, or rebirth, and the concept of Kamma, the law of cause and effect that never ceases until the cycle of birth-death-rebirth ends. Kamma is the accumulation of good and bad deeds of former lives to which a newborn individual falls heir. It is understood that a man is able to make a choice between doing right and wrong. If a person, or other being, chooses to do evil, he will have to make up for it in a future life. If he elects to do good, to "make merit" as the Thais say, he will continue slowly onward in his progression toward Nibbana, the end of the cycle of rebirth.

Many lifetimes are needed to achieve Nibbana. This inheritance, this Kamma, cannot be equated with a personality or a soul inhabiting one body after another. The force that continues resembles more a spark of energy flashing through the generations. In one lifetime, the circumstances will be dictated by the accumulation of virtue, or lack of it, in former lives. Similarly, future lives will be more or less comfortable according to one's conduct during this lifetime. Thus, one may be born into misery as the result of evil done many lives ago and hence must practice goodness in order to counteract the past. One must endure until at some final achievement perfection is reached, and with it an end to earthly existence. Then one must no longer suffer further rebirths, but instead may enjoy forever a degree of bliss unimaginable to human minds.

As one might at some time be born as a wild beast or other form of animal life, the early Indians felt a kinship with all living beings. Man identified with nature and saw oneness in every aspect of creation. The earth was thought to be populated by a host of imaginary animals and ghosts. Spirits inhabited trees, rocks, and streams. These remnants of the most primitive form of worship were accepted in Brahmanism. Many of the earth deities were subsequently incorporated into Buddhist myth and folktales.

The Indians, living on a low subcontinent with the towering snow-capped Himalayan peaks to the north, thought their world to be the southern part of one of four continents at the center of which was Mount Meru, the core of the universe. Their continent was called Jambudvipa, named for the *jambu,* or rose-apple, trees which grew there. As the great forest stretched toward the unknown impenetrable region of the Himalayas, it seemed to grow more strange and magical until it merged with the heavens of the gods on the tops of the high peaks. This mythical forest, the Himavat, frequently mentioned in the Jatakas, was peopled with both real and imaginary creatures.

Often they had magical powers. A horse might fly over the mountaintops; an elephant could bring prosperity to a kingdom by its very presence. A *kinnari,* a being with a woman's torso and head but the legs and wings of a bird, might serve helpless human beings and teach them to survive the perils of the forest. Here too roamed the mighty *nagas,* magical snakes that inhabited rich kingdoms below the earth. They were the spirits of the waters, so necessary for survival in a land dependent on the annual rainy season. Their archenemies were the *garudas,* giant birds that symbolized the sun and air. *Yakkhas* also appeared in the Himavat from time to time. Originally tree spirits, in the Jatakas they have become demonic giants, guardians of the riches of the earth.

In an effort to explain their universe, the early Buddhists devised a complex cosmology. This comprises three major spheres: lowest, the sphere of the senses; above it, the sphere of form, or intellect without sense perception; and highest, the sphere of the formless.

Lowest in the sphere of the senses is the underworld, which consists of four divisions: the various hells, inhabited by beings in torment; the animal kingdoms; the domain of ever-hungry ghosts called *petas;* and the realm of the *asuras,* or demons. Above these is the world of men, and above that are the six heavens of the inferior gods, or *devas.*

The second sphere, that of form without desire, contains sixteen Brahma heavens, each ruled by a Great Brahma with a material body. The highest sphere consists of four formless worlds where there is neither desire nor form, and here the Great Brahmas have no physical shape. Nibbana is beyond all this, unimaginable to mankind.

In the last ten Jataka tales, the worlds most often mentioned are the hells, the naga realm, the world of men, Tavatimsa heaven, and the Brahma heavens. Tavatimsa, one of the six heavens of the devas, is the realm of Indra, called Sakka by the Theravada Buddhists, and his thirty-three gods of Vedic origin. It is a splendid kingdom, inhabited by heavenly musicians called *gandhabbas* and beautiful dancers known as *apsaras.* There the devas live in crystal mansions and enjoy all manner of sensual delights.

Far above Tavatimsa are the Brahma heavens. Neither emotion nor desire for sensory pleasure remains, only the bliss of pure reason. It is to these heavens that men may aspire as a result of lives of great virtue.

The world seen in the following tales may appear fanciful and magical, but it is not without meaning. Each tale has an inner significance. Each individual has a role to play and a part in the resolution of events. Into the imaginative and colorful threads of the story a moral is woven. The ten great virtues are demonstrated, and the consequences of wrongdoing are made clear. Perhaps this happy mixture of lesson and fantasy explains why the Jatakas have survived for so many hundreds of years.

THE LAST TEN JATAKA TALES

with color photographs of Siamese temple paintings

A NOTE ON THE PAINTINGS

From the following plates it will be all too apparent that many of Siam's temple paintings have deteriorated badly. If this book should have the happy effect of encouraging the preservation the paintings cry for, the authors and photographer will feel well compensated for the many months of effort they have put into this endeavor.

I. TEMIYA THE MUTE PRINCE

(Illustrated on pages 27–28 and 33)

THERE ONCE LIVED a king of Benares who, despite all his riches and plenty, was, alas, unhappy. For though he possessed sixteen thousand wives, he had neither son nor daughter. Each and every one of his wives prayed zealously that she might bear a son to him. His chief queen, Candadevi, known for her virtues, asked of the great god Sakka, "If through my life I have done only good, may a son be born to me."

When her plea reached Tavatimsa heaven, the throne of Sakka, king of the gods, became warm—an infallible sign of an injustice on earth—and Sakka realized that he had overlooked the virtues of Queen Candadevi. Forthwith, from among the deities in heaven he chose the Bodhisatta, who he knew would serve as a model of self-denial for the kingdom of Benares, and sent him down to earth to be conceived in the queen's womb. In addition, to five hundred nobles' wives he sent five hundred more beings to be born as the Bodhisatta's attendants.

When the queen felt as though her womb contained a diamond, she knew she was with child. She informed the king, and both rejoiced. Great care was taken of her until the day of her delivery. Upon hearing the words "A son is born unto you, O King," the new father felt joy run through his veins and paternal affection lighten his heart. At the same time, true to Sakka's design, five hundred nobles' wives gave birth to infants who were to grow up with the Bodhisatta and serve him. The Bodhisatta was given sweet milk from sixty-four wet nurses selected because of their flawless beauty. After presenting the nurses to the queen the king felt generous and told her he would grant anything she asked. However, the queen postponed her request, preferring to wait for the day when she might need it.

23

On the occasion of the naming of the child, the Brahmins proclaimed that the royal son and heir to the throne possessed every mark of good fortune. The king named his son Temiya-Kumaro, meaning "prince drenched with water," because both his birth and the rainy day on which he was born were very wet.

When Temiya was only one month old, he was dressed up for his first public appearance and brought to the throne of his father to sit on his knee. Many courtiers admired his beauty and murmured their approval. Four robbers were then brought before the king to be judged. Temiya witnessed his father sentence one robber to a thousand strokes from thorn-baited whips, another to imprisonment in chains, a third to death by the spear, and a fourth to death by impaling. The infant Bodhisatta was terrified at his father's apparent cruelty and thought to himself, "Ah, a king acts as judge, and so my father must perform cruel actions every day. By condemning men to death or torture, he will himself be condemned to hell."

The next day, awakening from a short nap and looking up at the great white umbrella above him, the infant began to think of what it would mean to be king. These thoughts alarmed him, even more so as he remembered a previous existence in which he himself had reigned as king of Benares for twenty years. As a result of dread decisions forced upon him in the position of king, he had had to suffer eighty thousand years in hell. Now he was destined to become king again in the same city, again to suffer the same fate. This was more than he could bear, and his golden body trembled and turned pale. As he lay wondering if escape was possible, a goddess dwelling in the umbrella above him, who had been his mother in a former life, spoke soothingly to him:

> "Temi my child, let me help you.
> You must do as I advise:
> Pretend to be a crippled mute,
> Don't move your limbs or use your voice;
> Then will the people refuse to crown you king
> And you shall be free."

Pledging himself to follow the goddess's counsel, the Bodhisatta began at once to show signs of being different from the other five hundred children. While the others cried out for their milk, Temiya did not utter a sound. For the first year, his mother and nurses noticed with alarm that he neither cried nor slept, moved nor listened, though his body appeared normal. Knowing that he must feel hunger, they thought to force a sound from him by withholding his milk, at times by starving him for a whole day, but to no avail. In his second year, they tempted him with various cakes and sweetmeats over which the other children fought. But Temiya would say to himself, "Eat the cakes if you wish for hell," and thus abstain. All kinds of foods, fruits, and toys left him unmoved, though other children grabbed greedily at them.

When he was five, they tried to terrify him into speaking. He was placed in the center of a house thatched with palm leaves. A servant was then ordered to set fire to it. Where normal children would have run away shrieking, the Bodhisatta remained motionless and sat quietly as the fire came closer to him, until he was taken away by his attendants. At six, they let an elephant loose at him; at seven, they allowed serpents to coil about him. Still he remained unharmed and unmoved. In the following years, they showed him terrifying mimes, threatened him with swords, and made holes in four sides of a curtain around his bed and had conch players blast their sound through to him. They tried him with drums and sudden bright lamps in the middle of the night, but they failed to break his trance. Desperate, they covered him with molasses and allowed flies to cover and bite him, but he did not flinch. They forced him to remain unbathed, but his need for cleanliness did not overpower him. Pans of fire were placed under his bed, causing boils to break out on his body, but still he said to himself that hell was a hundred thousand times worse. His parents besought him to speak, to move, to listen, but he dared not.

At sixteen, when he would have been named heir apparent, they led him to a perfumed chamber and tried to tempt him with beautiful maidens, but he stopped himself from breathing in order not to be weakened by the fragrances.

At last, the king summoned the soothsayers and asked them why at his son's birth they had not mentioned any threatening signs of this affliction. Not understanding Temiya's behavior but unwilling to admit their ignorance, they explained that they had not dared cast a shadow on the king's joy when, after so many years, he had been given a son. But now, fearing for the safety of the country should an apparent idiot be named heir to the throne, they fabricated predictions foretelling of dangers to the king's life if Temiya were allowed to remain in the kingdom. Alarmed by their words, the king asked what he should do. They advised him in this way: "You must yoke some unlucky horses to an unlucky chariot, send your son away in it, passing by the western gate, to a graveyard, and there he must be buried."

When the queen heard of this plot, she knew the time had come to make the request which the king had promised years ago to grant. "Give the kingdom to my son," she demanded. "For once he is crowned, he will certainly speak."

The king protested. "Impossible, my Queen, for your son brings ill luck to us."

"Then give it to him for seven years," she responded.

Again the king refused.

"Then for seven months," she pleaded.

"O Queen," he said, "I dare not."

"Then, alas, for seven days," she sighed.

"Very well." The king relented. "Your wish is granted."

And so it happened that Temiya was given the kingdom for seven days. He was led around the city, sometimes on an elephant, sometimes on men's shoulders. Still he would not move either his limbs or his lips. On the seventh day, his mother begged him to speak, for on the morrow he was condemned to die. The Bodhisatta gravely considered her request, thinking to himself: "If I do not break my silence, my mother's own heart will break; if I do, I shall have wasted in one second what efforts I have made for sixteen years. Moreover, if I keep my pledge, my parents and I shall be saved from hell." Thus, Temiya again decided to be patient and await his release from that household. For the day was near when he would be freed from the fear of inheriting the throne, and on that day, he would be able to speak.

As the next morning dawned, the king gave his final orders to Sunanda the charioteer. "Yoke some ill-omened horses to an ill-omened chariot and set the prince in it. Take him out the western gate and find ground in which to dig a grave. After you have dug the hole, throw him into it and break his head with the back of your spade to kill him. Then scatter dust over him and make a heap of earth above. After bathing yourself, come hither."

Sunanda took Temiya off, but though he thought he was passing through the western gate, the Death Gate, he did in fact drive to the eastern gate, which was the Victory Gate, and one of the chariot's wheels struck the threshold. At the

PLATE 1 (*facing page*). THE TEMIYA JATAKA, *overall view (Wat Yai Intharam, Chon-buri): a) Temiya Witnesses His Father's Judgment b) Attempt to Frighten Temiya with a Wild Elephant c) Attempt to Frighten Temiya with Snake and Sword d) Temiya Tests His Strength e) The King Visits Temiya at His Hermitage.*

For further comments, see page 134 and the commentaries on plates 2–4.

sound, the Bodhisatta knew he was on the threshold of attaining his freedom. By the power of the gods, a graveyard appeared. Sunanda stopped and removed Temiya's royal ornaments from him, releasing him in one stroke from his yoke of royalty.

The Bodhisatta was at last freed from his vow, and as Sunanda worked at digging the grave, Temiya thought to himself, "In sixteen years, I have never moved my hands or feet. Can I do so now?" Whereupon he rose, rubbed his hands together, rubbed his feet with his hands, and alighted onto the ground, which at his touch became like a cushion filled with air. He then exercised his limbs by walking back and forth until he was satisfied that he had the strength he thought he had lost.

This was his only chance to escape kingship and enter the forest as an ascetic, and the Bodhisatta wondered, was he powerful enough to overcome Sunanda if he tried to prevent his escape? As a final test of his strength, the Bodhisatta seized the back of the chariot and lifted it high with one hand as if it were a toy cart. Indeed, his power was confirmed. He walked over to the charioteer and tried to jolt him into looking at him with these words:

PLATE 2 (*facing page, top*). THE TEMIYA JATAKA (*Wat Yai Intharam, Chonburi*): *Temiya Witnesses His Father's Judgment of the Criminals.*

A courtyard bounded by a crenellated wall contains the men to be judged by the king. Their bodies form orbs of various sizes and shapes, while their heads are shaved so far above the ears as to make their hair resemble small caps.

For further comments, see pages 134 and 136.

PLATE 3 (*facing page, bottom*). THE TEMIYA JATAKA (*Wat Yai Intharam, Chonburi*): *a) Temiya Tests His Strength by Lifting the Chariot b) The King Visits Temiya at His Hermitage.*

Encircled by trees and rocks, these two scenes take place at the uppermost part of the painting (see Plate 1). In the first scene, Temiya's strength is confirmed by his lifting the chariot. For further details, see the commentary on Plate 4.

In the second scene, Temiya has taken the vows of an ascetic and lives in a hut in the forest. With one hand raised and the other holding a monk's fan, he preaches to his father the king, who kneels before him, his palms held together. Men from the king's entourage can be seen huddled near the trees behind him.

For further comments on these two scenes, see pages 134 and 137.

"Behold the man you seek to kill, not deaf nor dumb nor lame;
Stop or bear the wrath of hell, for by this act you'll die."

Sunanda looked up but was so dazzled by the Bodhisatta's beauty that he did not recognize him at first. Again Temiya identified himself. Suddenly Sunanda understood and fell at his feet, stammering that he would be honored to escort the prince home to inherit the kingdom. He who was destined for Buddhahood chided him, for nothing would deter him now from leading the pure meditative life. He described his previous existence and subsequent generations in hell and then ordered Sunanda to return to the palace immediately to tell his parents that he was still alive and thus spare them unnecessary grief over the loss of their only son.

As the charioteer approached the palace alone, the queen, who had been waiting by a window, saw him, assumed that her son was dead, and began to weep. But when Sunanda told her his story, she ceased. The king was told what his son had done, and he and the queen set out at once for the Victory Gate, hoping to lure the prince home.

When the long procession of horse-drawn carriages came to a halt, the royal pair found their son living in a hut of leaves prepared for him by Sakka. They saw that he had already put on an ascetic's garments of red bark and leopard skin, a black antelope skin over one shoulder and a carrying pole over the other. His hair was tied up and matted, and he held a walking staff in one hand. Temiya welcomed them and explained to them the reasons for his sixteen years of self-denial. In awe of their son, they no longer begged him to wear the crown but were themselves inspired to embrace the holy life. Returning to the palace, the king ordered the royal treasure jars to be opened and the gold to be scattered about like sand. Sakka built for the entire kingdom a hermitage three leagues long, so that all who aspired to Nibbana could partake of the meditative life.

II. MAHAJANAKA THE LOST PRINCE

(Illustrated on pages 34 and 39)

THERE ONCE WAS a king, Mahajanaka, of Mithila in the kingdom of Videha. He had two sons, Aritthajanaka and Polajanaka. When the old king died, the elder brother, Aritthajanaka, became king, and the younger brother his viceroy. In time the new king became suspicious of his brother's popularity with the people and, fearful for his throne, had Polajanaka put in chains. But when Polajanaka proclaimed his innocence, miraculously his chains fell off and he was able to escape to a small village near the frontier of the kingdom. Since he was a strong leader, he attracted many followers. In time he decided to take his revenge by declaring war on King Aritthajanaka.

Before the king went to battle with his brother, he made his pregnant wife promise that should he be killed, she would flee from Mithila in order to protect the unborn child. When she heard of the king's death at the hand of his brother, Polajanaka, she gathered her gold and jewels into a basket and covered them with rice. She put on some worn and dirty garments and blackened her face with soot so that she would not be recognized. Then, lifting the basket onto her head, she went unnoticed out of the city by the northern gate.

Now, the child in the fleeing queen's womb was to be a Great Being, or Bodhisatta, and the attention of Sakka, king of the gods, was drawn to the queen's plight. He therefore attired himself as an old man driving a carriage; on arriving at the queen's side, he asked her where she was bound. She had in mind to go to the city of Kalacampa, sixty leagues distant, but did not know the way. The disguised god offered to take her there, and after entering the carriage, the queen fell into a heavy sleep. By nightfall the carriage had reached the edge of Kalacampa. When the amazed queen asked how they could have reached the city so soon, Sakka told her that he had come by a straight road known only to the gods, then departed.

In Kalacampa, the unrecognized queen was observed by a northern Brahmin teacher of great fame. When he asked who she might be, she told him, "The chief queen of King Aritthajanaka of Mithila, lately killed in battle. I have come here in order to save the life of my unborn child."

The Brahmin invited her to live in his house, saying that he would watch over her as if she were his younger sister. The queen agreed, and a short time later she was delivered of a son, whom she called after his grandfather Mahajanaka. He grew into a strong and sturdy child. However, he was often teased by his playmates and called "the widow's son," which name brought questions to his mind regarding his paternity. One day he went to his mother, threatening to bite off her breasts if she did not tell him who his father was. She was forced to reveal to him the secret of his birth—that he was the son of the former king of Mithila.

When the boy reached the age of sixteen, he determined to regain his father's kingdom. He told his mother of his plan and she offered to give him her gold and jewels, which were sufficient to win back the kingdom. But he took only half of her gift, wishing to make his fortune in trade. She was alarmed for his safety, warning him of the dangers of the sea, but he was deaf to her words. After purchasing some goods for trading, he boarded a vessel bound for Suvannabhumi, the golden land of the east. On that day his uncle Polajanaka, king of Mithila, fell ill.

Crowded on board were the men and animals from seven large caravans. After seven days of plunging through the heavy seas at top speed, the overloaded ship began to founder. Planks broke off, and the water rose higher and higher. Mahajanaka, knowing that the ship was sinking, did not panic. He prepared himself for the ordeal by eating a full meal, covered himself with sugar and ghee to protect himself from the water, then tied himself to the mast. When the ship went down, men and animals were devoured by the sharks and fierce turtles that

PLATE 4 (*facing page*). THE TEMIYA JATAKA (*Wat Yai Intharam, Chonburi*): *Temiya Tests His Strength by Lifting the Chariot.*

Temiya's raising the chariot causes the horses hitched to it to twist their necks around and shocks the gravedigger into looking up. According to the Pali text of this story, the gravedigger does not see Temiya at this point; he continues to dig. The painter here has chosen to ignore this fact in favor of artistic unity.

For further comments, see pages 134, 136, and 137.

ข อันนี้พระมะหาธะนึกไปตกเสียเรือ
ลิงวายน้ำนองเมกขาหลามอุ้มไป

infested the ocean, but the mast remained upright. Mahajanaka with his superior strength was able to throw himself a distance of 140 cubits from the ship, thus escaping the fate of the other passengers. On that day Polajanaka died, leaving the throne of Mithila vacant.

Mahajanaka floated in the ocean for seven days, taking no food. During this time the goddess Manimekhala was enjoying the pleasures of heaven, neglecting her duties as guardian of the seas. At last she spied him and recognized that he was not an ordinary mortal. She took him in her arms, and Mahajanaka, thrilled by the touch of the goddess, fell into a trance. She flew with him to a mango grove in the kingdom of Mithila, where she laid him on his right side on a ceremonial stone in the middle of the grove.

From his deathbed, the king of Mithila had told his ministers that to find a man

PLATE 5 (*facing page, top*). THE MAHAJANAKA JATAKA (*Wat Bang Yi Khan, Thonburi*): *King Aritthajanaka Battles with His Brother, Polajanaka.*

This scene represents the battle that took place before Mahajanaka's birth between his father the king and his uncle. The winner, his uncle, is seen in profile lunging at his opponent, whose royal umbrella breaks and whose soldiers, in awkward postures, scamper over one another in fear and flight. The point at which the pale blue sky and grayish ground meet suggests a horizon line, but it has no depth. The battle appears to float against sky and earth, above trees and rocks.

PLATE 6 (*facing page, bottom*). THE MAHAJANAKA JATAKA (*Wat No, Suphanburi*): *a) Mahajanaka Is Shipwrecked b) Mahajanaka Is Rescued by the Goddess Manimekhala.*

Two events that take place seven days apart are represented side by side here. The first is when Mahajanaka looks up from the sea at Manimekhala before she swoops down to save him. The Bodhisatta and the goddess seem to float, the former against waves, the latter against sky, while the less fortunate sailors, having jumped or tumbled from the capsizing clipper ship, are swallowed up by the sea or ferocious fish. The lower half of the goddess is a profile view of bent legs and fan-shaped skirt, in contrast with the upper half, a three-quarter view.

In the second scene, Manimekhala cradles the sleeping Mahajanaka in her arms on the way to the mango grove. The Thai inscription reads: "Mahajanaka is shipwrecked, swims in the water, the deva Mekhala carries him away."

For further comments, see pages 135 and 137.

worthy of being king, they must look for one who could answer certain riddles, who could string the king's powerful bow, and who could please his daughter, the beautiful and intelligent Princess Sivali. There were many candidates for the throne. Each one, in an effort to win Sivali, obeyed her every whim. The more they tried to please her, the more she scorned them and sent them away. Moreover, not one had the wit to answer the riddles or the strength to string the royal bow.

At length the ministers decided to send out the festive chariot to see if they could find a successor to Polajanaka. They decorated the city, yoked four noble steeds to the handsome carriage, and bade the musicians follow behind as is proper when a royal chariot is empty. Then they ordered the carriage to lead them to the one who had sufficient merit to be king of Mithila. Followed by a great crowd, it took them through the city to the eastern gate and onward to the park where Mahajanaka lay sleeping. After circling the stone, the chariot came to a stop. The ministers observed the sleeping prince and examined his feet, whereby they recognized the signs of royalty. Indeed, they saw that he was not only a future king but also destined to be emperor of four continents. They commanded the musicians to sound their instruments. At the noise, Mahajanaka awoke. Seeing the multitudes around him, he recognized that the white umbrella of kingship had come to him. He asked where the king might be; when told that he had died, he agreed to accept the kingdom.

Meanwhile, Princess Sivali was waiting. However, when the new king arrived he did not visit her or pay her any attention. One day when he was strolling in the garden, she could bear his indifference no longer. Running up to offer him her arm to lean on, she showed that he pleased her. Shortly thereafter she became his queen.

King Mahajanaka answered the riddles with ease. He was also able through his great strength to string the bow of King Polajanaka, so that he fulfilled all the conditions for becoming king. Wisely and well he ruled for seven thousand years. His wife Sivali bore him a son and heir to the throne.

One day the king was riding through his kingdom with his ministers when he observed two mango trees. The one that had been full of mangoes was broken and torn by the people who had come to pick the fruit, while the other, though barren, stood green and whole. Thus he came to understand that possessions bring only sorrow, and he determined to put aside his kingdom and take up the life of an ascetic. After shaving his head and putting on the robes of a hermit, he departed from the palace. But Queen Sivali, who loved him, followed him with a great retinue. Wherever he went, she was behind him. At last he could bear it no longer. He cut a stalk of grass and said to her, "As this reed cannot be joined again, so you and I can never be joined again."

At his words, Sivali fell down in a swoon. While the courtiers were attending to her, Mahajanaka disappeared into the forest. When the queen awoke, she could find him nowhere. He was never again seen in the world of men, for he found his way to the Himavat forest and eventually entered the Brahma heaven.

The despairing queen returned to Mithila and arranged for the coronation of her son. Having settled the affairs of the kingdom, she herself donned the robes of a hermit, and after many years she too was deemed worthy of entrance into the kingdom of the gods.

PLATE 7 *(page 39).* THE MAHAJANAKA JATAKA *(Wat Phuthaisawan, Ayuthaya): Brahmin Ministers Recognize the Sleeping Mahajanaka as Their Future King.*

The sleeping Prince Mahajanaka is recognized as king by Brahmin ministers from the court of his late uncle, who have sent a riderless royal chariot out to discover a new king. Mahajanaka is found reclining, with one hand supporting his head, on a pedestal with a coverlet and lionlike legs. His left arm repeats the curve of his side. A tree shades him. Below the pedestal, the ministers kneel and join hands in reverence to their newfound king. To the right of them are musicians playing wind instruments. Part of the bow-shaped tail of the chariot is seen to the right of the sleeper.

This is one of the few recognizable fragments of murals of the last ten Jataka stories in the Patriarch's residence at Wat Phuthaisawan.

For further comments, see pages 131 and 136.

III. SAMA THE DEVOTED SON

(Illustrated on pages 40 and 45)

ON OPPOSITE BANKS of a river dividing the kingdom of Benares lay two villages. Their hunter chiefs, fast friends throughout the years, betrothed their infant children to each other shortly after their birth. Now, these two were not like other children; they were born with skins of golden hue. And although they were surrounded by hunters, they refused to harm any living crea-

PLATE 8 *(facing page)*. THE MAHAJANAKA AND SAMA JATAKAS *(Wat No, Suphanburi):* *a) Manimekhala Takes Leave of Mahajanaka in the Mango Grove b) King Piliyakka Informs Sama's Parents of His Deed c) Sama's Parents Mourn Their Son's Apparent Death.*

Three scenes from two different stories are portrayed here against the same forest background. In the upper left-hand portion of the picture, Manimekhala places Mahajanaka on a stone slab in a mango grove. An inscription under the scene reads: "The deva Mekhala carries Mahajanaka and places him here." The lowermost inscription summarizes this portion of the Sama Jataka: "Sama is hit by the arrow and falls dead. Piliyakka goes to tell Sama's father and mother to come claim their son's body and place it in a sheltered spot." The scene of King Piliyakka kneeling before Sama's parents is in the lower right-hand part of the picture. The inscription here reads: "This is the house where Sama's father and mother live." Below and to the left Sama is being mourned. The difference between the lamenting postures of the parents and the seated king shows that the king is an intruder and does not belong in the quiet Himavat. The inscription above this scene explains the presence of a deva in a tree: "This is the deva who descends to help bring Sama back to life and cure the parents' blindness."

Different areas of the painting are unified by a decorative, nonrealistic use of color. For further comments, see page 134.

ture. Theirs was a special destiny, for they had to replace with purity and goodness an evil carried with them from a former life. At that time, many lives ago,
they had been born into the family of a doctor who, angered by a rich patient's
refusal to pay his fee for curing the eye disease, gave him some medicine which
took away the sight of one eye. Though the evil was done by the head of that
household, the children of the family also had to do penance. Thus it was that,
once they were born into families of hunters and betrothed, they felt obliged
to live as ascetics and deny themselves all pleasures of the senses. In vain each
begged his parents to forgo the nuptials. Against their will they were married
but secretly determined to live as brother and sister.

Dukulaka, as the boy was called, and Parika, the girl, unwilling to hunt or
partake of the comforts of their parents' dwelling, were allowed to go into the
forest and live in a hermitage where they led lives of meditation and purity.
Although Sakka helped them with their small needs, he was uneasy, for he knew
that their past had not yet been washed clean. Sakka foresaw that a grave misfortune was to strike them. He tried to convince them that they would have to bear
a son in order to be assured of someone to care for them when affliction struck.
"Never," they said. "Impossible." For this was not the way of asceticism. At last
Sakka persuaded them that a pure conception could take place if, at the proper
time, Dukulaka placed one finger on his wife's navel.

So it was that the Bodhisatta was reborn into the world of men. But it was not
quite a human world. As the ascetics came and went, looking for berries and nuts
in the forest, it was the graceful kinnaris who looked after Suvannasama, or Sama,
as the Bodhisatta was named at birth. This holy life could only have taken place in
the Himavat forest, below the peaks that reach into the very palaces of the gods
in Sakka's heaven. And yet, its inhabitants were not immune to danger. When
Sama was sixteen, as predicted, a misfortune befell his parents. As they were
making their way home after a day of gathering fruits, it suddenly began to rain.
Taking shelter at the roots of a tree, they unwittingly stood on an anthill under
which a poisonous snake resided. As they huddled there, drops of their sweat fell
onto the snake and he was angered. So he puffed out his deadly breath at them
and blinded them instantly.

From this time onward their son, whom they grew to cherish even more than
before, was their sole support. Sama tied ropes and bamboo poles in all directions for them to follow. He swept their dwelling clean of leaves and insects, collected their food, fed them succulent fruits, went every day to a pond to fill a
waterpot for them. He bathed them and comforted them. He moved about so

gently that even the deer, timid of other men, were never afraid of him and accompanied him wherever he went.

One evening, while Sama was fetching the evening's water in his small round pot, which one of the deer that accompanied him used to carry for him, the king of Benares himself wandered into the forest. While hunting for venison, he had chanced upon a glade near the pond where Sama stood. The king, named Piliyakka, was fascinated by the sight of what appeared to be some divine creature for his ability to tame the animals of the forest. He was consumed with curiosity and the desire to take a trophy home to show his ministers. Envisioning the reception he would enjoy once he returned home with such a prize, Piliyakka in his pride drew back his bow and shot a poisoned arrow into Sama's side. The deer fled in terror. The waterpot tumbled over. And Sama slowly and gravely sank to the sand. Blood poured from his lips as he spoke aloud, asking who it could be who desired his death and what could be gained by such an act.

King Piliyakka was struck by the absence of blame or anger in Sama's words and ventured out of concealment. As they talked, the king pretended that he had been aiming at one of the deer rather than at Sama. But Sama knew this to be a lie, and Piliyakka had to admit the truth. Still the boy did not reprimand him. Instead, he grieved aloud for his parents. Who would feed them now? Who would bring them water each day? Who would bathe them? The king was struck with shame. Whereupon he took up the waterpot and promised Sama to care for his parents as if they were his own. Sama then lost consciousness. Piliyakka, thinking he was dead, wailed loudly and paid homage to Sama's body.

In the meantime, a daughter of the gods who had been Sama's mother in his seventh incarnation before this one sensed that something had befallen her former son. Convinced that Sama as well as his parents would die if she did not intercede, she proceeded to the scene and, hidden in a tree, spoke to the king, who had already begun to change his mind about caring for Sama's parents. "O king," she admonished him. "You have done a grievous thing. Go and nurse the blind parents and your bad deed shall be forgotten. Be charitable of heart and you will attain heaven."

Inspired by the goddess's words, Piliyakka set out for the hermitage. There he confessed his crime to Sama's parents. They were stricken with sorrow and grief. So great was their suffering that their penance, carried with them throughout so many lifetimes, was at that moment ended. Unaware of their renewed purity, they asked merely that the king lead them to their son's body. The king reluctantly complied.

On reaching their son, the two ascetics knelt down and wept. All past evils having been washed away by their tears, they were able to bring their son back to life. As his mother prayed, Sama's body slowly turned to one side. As his father took up his mother's solemn words, he turned to the other side. The goddess, who had witnessed these acts from her hiding place, then revealed herself and profoundly asserted the virtue of Sama. The air was tense. Even the kinnaris who had cared for Sama as a child gathered quietly to wait for a miracle to happen.

Through the night they remained beside him, all minds bent on restoring life to the boy who seemed more a heavenly being than a human. At last Sama stirred, then rose, fully recovered from his injury. At that very moment, dawn broke over the forest and Sama's mother and father could see with their own eyes Sama's restoration, for their blindness had ended along with their penance. King Piliyakka, who had come as an intruder into this quiet and pure world, left the site, full of wonder and amazement at the miraculous event he had witnessed. He was unaware to the last that even he had served as an agent of good, for without his cruel act, the devoted son Sama could not have ended his parents' affliction.

PLATE 9 (*facing page, top*). THE SAMA JATAKA (*Wat Yai Intharam, Chonburi*): *King Piliyakka Shoots Sama*.

The scene of King Piliyakka shooting an arrow into Sama's side is surrounded by attractive landscape details of brown and green hues. The lotus pond in the foreground is given depth along a zigzagging diagonal line; it leads the eye directly into the scene, in the direction of the arrow. Sama has both hands on the waterpot as the deer flee.

For further comments, see pages 136 and 137.

PLATE 10 (*facing page, bottom*). THE SAMA JATAKA (*Wat Bang Yi Khan, Thonburi*): *King Piliyakka, Sama's Parents, a Goddess, and Kinnari Maidens Lament over Sama's Body*.

After the king has led Sama's parents to their son's body, they are joined in lamentation by a goddess and two kinnaris (seen in the foreground). Leopard-skin garments and bark-spired crowns indicate the ascetic mode of dress of Sama and his parents. One kinnari is seen from the back, side, and three-quarter view all at once.

For further comments, see pages 134 and 136.

IV. NIMI THE NOBLE KING

(Illustrated on pages 46 and 129)

THERE ONCE LIVED a king named Makhadeva, who upon spying his first gray hair told his barber to pluck it out and put it in his hand. When the barber asked him why, he replied solemnly, "This gray hair is a messenger from the heavens. Four and eighty thousand years I have passed as a youth. Four and eighty thousand years I have been king. The time has come for me to renounce my throne and the worldly life, and to live the life of an ascetic eighty-four thousand more years." True to his word, King Makhadeva handed his kingdom over to his son, charging him to be alert to his first gray hair so that he too could take up the hermit's life and give the kingdom to his own son. And so it happened. Son after son after son of the line of King Makhadeva reigned until the sign of the first gray

PLATE 11 *(facing page).* THE NIMI JATAKA, *overall view (Wat Yai Intharam, Chonburi): a) Nimi Preaches to the Devas in Tavatimsa Heaven   b) Nimi Visits the Various Hells.*

Tavatimsa heaven and the hells are separated horizontally by a jagged line. From his chariot in the worlds of hell, Nimi points to the creatures of hell, who appear as rubbery ghosts of human beings. They are shocked by the light brought into their dark world by Nimi and the golden chariot.

Sakka's heaven, far from the hells and earth, is more orderly, with flying and seated devas arranged in a loose symmetry, their hands joined in reverence to Nimi. The red backdrop, dotted with falling three-petaled flowers, is a typical Ayuthaya-period way to paint heaven. Flowers symbolize the conferring of blessings. Sakka, Brahma, and two other figures below Nimi are kneeling in front of a flowered screen.

For further comments, see pages 134 and 137.

hair, then exchanged kingship for asceticism and, like their forefathers, upon death entered the heaven of pure intellect, Brahma's heaven.

Eighty-four thousand generations minus two passed, and King Makhadeva, from his place in Brahma's heaven, was pleased that all his descendants had followed his example. Then he pondered, "Will any of us attain Nibbana now?" He perceived that the state of nonbeing was not within the reach of any of his line. This being the case, Makhadeva resolved to round off his family line by coming to earth again as the son of his descendant the present king of Mithila. In this way he would be reborn as a king, bear one more son to whom he would give his throne, and become an ascetic once again. Then, after his death, he would watch his childless son turn to the holy life and finally end the cycle of Makhadeva's family.

When Makhadeva descended from Brahma's heaven, he was born as a Bodhisatta, and the soothsayers correctly foresaw that he was meant to round off his family. Hearing this, the king named his newborn son after the hoop of a chariot wheel. The Bodhisatta was called Nimi-Kumara, or Prince Hoop. According to tradition, when his father caught sight of his first gray hair young Prince Nimi became king.

As king, Nimi was faultless, ruling by example, giving alms, caring for the poor as if they were his own kinsmen, and observing in earnest the holy days. Indeed, he inspired many of his people to lead such good lives that upon death they reached the realm of Sakka's heaven.

Now King Nimi, like all truly good men, was not satisfied with himself and yearned to know the answer to one great question: which is more fruitful, the holy life or faithful almsgiving? So strong was his desire to learn the truth that Sakka's throne became warm and the king of the gods sped in person to Nimi's chamber. The palace became like a fiery light as Sakka entered and explained: "Good King Nimi, I have come to help answer your question. The holy life, in which a man lives as an ascetic, is by far the more fruitful, for by meditating he can go beyond my heaven, where we gods still have senses and feelings, to Brahma's heaven, where only the intellect remains, and sometimes beyond that, to Nibbana. Nevertheless, almsgiving to all, regardless of caste, is right and befits a great man and a king such as you, King Nimi." Without further delay Sakka departed, leaving Nimi pondering his words.

When Sakka reached his home, Tavatimsa heaven, he described at length the good and pious King Nimi to the deities. They were overjoyed to hear of him, for some of them were former subjects of his, and they cried, "Let us see him! We wish to look upon him again, for at one time from his very own lips we received his teachings, and through his example we attained godhood." They persuaded the great Sakka to agree.

And so he ordered the divine chariot to appear and be readied for a journey to earth. Matali the charioteer was called upon to guide the chariot, pulled by one thousand thoroughbred steeds, to earth to bring King Nimi back to heaven to stand before the gods.

On the festival of the full moon, after traveling earthward for many days, the chariot appeared over the city of Mithila in the kingdom of Videha, whose people were still celebrating though it was late at night. Catching sight of the celestial chariot as it shone above their heads in the sky, they marveled at it and wondered what it might be. A second moon? A sign from heaven on this festival day? When they saw that it was a chariot, they realized that it must be Sakka's own vehicle come to their king, whose righteousness had caught the eye of the gods.

Matali guided the chariot to the eastern window of the palace, where King Nimi was seated contemplating; and as the moon rose in the east, Matali called out, "King Nimi! The deities of Sakka's heaven are well pleased with you and are longing to see you. I am sent by the king of the gods himself to escort you to his realm."

King Nimi accepted graciously, but before entering the chariot, he told his people that he would not be gone long. As they rose into the sky, Matali asked him which road he would like to take first, the one to heaven or the one to hell. Nimi, knowing that whatever befell him, he would always be able to see heaven, chose the road to hell, saying, "Take me first to the bowels of the universe, to hell, where the condemned dwell."

Matali plunged the chariot into the blackness of the various worlds of hell. Fires blazed, and soon they saw below them the burning River Vetarani, covered with brine that erodes the flesh, emitting the most fetid odors, and filled with struggling sinners. Nimi wept to see such suffering and cried out to Matali, "O Matali, what did those men do to be cast into such a river?" Matali told him in what ways they had been cruel and how their wrongdoing had begotten other evils.

Then Matali made this river disappear and summoned the next hell to appear, where misers and men who had been selfish with ascetics and Brahmins were being torn by black dogs, crows, and vultures. Nimi shook and shuddered to see still another hell where those who had tormented other people were being pounded with hot lumps of coal, and another where perjurers and debtors struggled to climb out of a fiery pit. At the sight of the hell where animal haters struggled head-down in iron caldrons filled with boiling water or fire, Nimi was filled with fear and horror. But Matali was unrelenting. He was determined to show Nimi all the hells: the one where dishonest grain sellers lay prostrate with heat, having been given water which instantly turned to chaff as they drank; the one where spears and arrows were plunged into the sides of men who had stolen and cheated others; the one where animal slayers were torn to shreds. Farther on, Nimi had to witness malicious men being forced to eat filth and garbage and those who had committed patricide and matricide drinking from a river of blood. Still farther on, greedy hagglers struggled like fish on hooks which pierced their tongues. Adulterous women wailed and waved their arms hopelessly, their upper halves in flames, their lower halves buried in mud. Still others strained endlessly to climb out of hell's windows, only to fall again and again. And Nimi grieved for them all that their evil deeds had brought them to this.

Meanwhile, the deities in Sakka's heaven wondered why Nimi was so long in coming. "Matali is wasting Nimi's lifetime visiting all the hells," they cried. "Tell him to hurry." Sakka sent a speedy messenger down to hell. When he finally reached them, he called out to Matali, "Show the king all the hells at once, that this visit be ended straightaway. The gods are impatient and are afraid you are using up Nimi's lifetime." Thus Matali opened all the worlds of hell to Nimi's sight, then turned the chariot heavenward and rushed the shocked Nimi away, his mind dazed by the horrors he had witnessed.

Swiftly the vehicle rose, passing heavenly mansions of great beauty, allowing Nimi to catch brief fragrances of gardens which perfumed the air, to glimpse crystal palaces which sparkled like gems, and to hear strains of cool celestial music sung by sweet nymphs and birds. To Nimi, each heavenly abode seemed more beautiful than the last, and at each he engaged Matali in conversation, asking, "What good did this mortal do in his earthly existence? Who was he that he attained such a celestial state?" Matali explained that the man who lived in seven mansions with his wives had in his lifetime given seven hermitages to seven hermits, that the women who dwelt in palaces of crystal with hundreds of columns, bells and banners, flowers and lakes, had been women who had always kept the holy days. He described how still others, who lived in mansions of gems filled with heavenly musicians playing lutes and singing, had fed holy men and provided their cities with parks and wells.

Once again, Matali's thoroughness in answering Nimi's questions annoyed the deities in heaven until they pressed Sakka into sending yet another swift messenger to hurry them along. "No more delay," cried the messenger. "Show Nimi all the heavenly mansions at once." After Matali opened up the heavens to Nimi's vision, he urged the horses on faster and faster.

Upward the carriage rose, past the seven hills surrounding Mount Sineru, past the heaven of the Four Great Kings, until at last, within sight of the huge statues of Sakka himself that framed the Cittakuta gateway to his heaven, Matali slowed the chariot with its one thousand steeds to a halt. As he led the chariot to a side platform on which he could land, Matali pointed out the eight-sided columns made of rare gems that supported the palace and announced to Nimi, "This is Tavatimsa, the heaven of the thirty-three; here the gods assemble, all thirty-three of them, with their master Sakka, the king, who looks after men and gods alike, permitting some to enter his heaven, others to remain, sending still others to hell. It is a beauteous and most sensual place, O King, as you shall see."

As they alighted, the deities ran to the gateway to greet Nimi with flowers and perfumes. The mighty Sakka begged him to be seated on his own throne and to stay to enjoy the delights of his heaven. Nimi, however, replied that he came not for unearned pleasures but for discussion of the moral precepts. For seven days Nimi charmed the company of heaven with his discourse, and at the end of that time, he again refused Sakka's invitation to remain. He felt that his people needed him. "Now I must depart," he said. "My subjects await me."

Once again the chariot was prepared and Matali summoned. Nimi bade the gods a friendly farewell and began his journey back to Mithila. When the chariot came in view of the city, the people again looked up wonderingly. Then, recognizing their king within it, they cried out with joy. Matali drove the chariot around the city once, put Nimi down at the eastern window of the palace, and departed for Sakka's realm. As King Nimi the Bodhisatta alighted, his subjects surrounded him and questioned him. Nimi told them of the wonders he had seen and of the peaceful existence of all who dwell in heaven. He also told them of the horrors he had witnessed in the underworld.

"Do good," he advised them. "Be charitable and of a pure heart, and you shall be reborn someday to such a heaven. Some of this kingdom's own people did I see there who, having done good in this city, have become deities in Sakka's heaven. All of you can attain that. But beware of evildoing, for I have seen in the worlds of hell more suffering and torture than my tongue can describe."

Years later, when the king's barber showed Nimi his first gray hair, Nimi knew it was time to give his kingdom to his son. From then on, he lived as an ascetic in a mango grove at Mithila and upon his death surpassed Sakka's heaven to enter the Brahma heaven, where all is mind and wisdom. Thus it was that Nimi, as the Bodhisatta, rounded off King Makhadeva's line and with the death of his son ended the cycle in the four and eighty thousandth generation.

V. MAHOSADHA THE CLEVER SAGE

(Illustrated on pages 57–60)

IN THE KINGDOM of Mithila ruled a king called Vedeha, who was instructed in the ways of the law by four sages. At dawn one morning the king was awakened by a fantastic and frightening dream. His whole world had been illumined by fire which rose in four columns from the corners of the world. Suddenly in the center a fifth flame arose, which was at first only the size of a firefly. As King Vedeha watched, the fifth flame grew in height and glory until it encompassed all the other pillars of fire. At the same time multitudes of people passed through the flames without harm. Terrified, the king consulted his sages about the meaning of such a scene.

The four wise men interpreted the dream to mean that a fifth sage would soon appear who would surpass them all. They themselves represented the four original columns of fire, and they saw in the dream their fame consumed by the growing splendor of the fifth and central flame. And, in fact, on that day a Bodhisatta, or future Buddha, was conceived in the womb of Lady Sumana, the wife of a wealthy merchant in the market town at the east gate of Mithila. At the same instant, a thousand other sons of the gods were conceived in the families of other rich men so that the Bodhisatta would be properly attended. Nine months later, the Lady Sumana brought forth a child the color of gold who was called Mahosadha. In his hand he clasped a medicinal herb which caused a painless birth for his mother and which cured all the sick who had gathered to see this marvelous infant.

Throughout his childhood Mahosadha grew in wisdom. At the age of seven he demonstrated the architectural talents which would later save both his kingdom and his king from destruction. He built a great hall with many rooms and surrounded it with lakes covered with lotus blossoms. There he would sit dispensing advice to petitioners who needed aid. And his childhood was a happy and peaceful time in all the kingdom, for a Bodhisatta had made his appearance.

Recalling his dream, King Vedeha decided to fetch Mahosadha to his court. The four sages were sent to find him, but they too remembered the prophecy and were reluctant to hasten their own fall from authority. They were so overcome with jealousy that they plotted ceaselessly to keep the Bodhisatta away. Each sage devised trials and riddles intended to prevent Mahosadha from reaching the king's presence. However, the boy solved whatever was set before him with great cleverness and at last had to be admitted to the court.

For many years Mahosadha instructed the king in matters both spiritual and temporal. At the same time, he had to be on guard constantly against the devious tricks of the old sages. However, he was able to thwart their jealous maneuvering and firmly directed King Vedeha into proper behavior, despite the king's childish tendency to believe whatever he was told and to obey his impulses regardless of the consequences.

During these years one hundred and one kings of India united under the leadership of a wicked sage called Kevatta and set out to conquer the whole of India. However, Mahosadha had not been idle. He had rebuilt Mithila's defenses and had sent spies to live among Kevatta's men, so that he was prepared to meet each challenge as it arose. When the kings laid siege to Mithila, Mahosadha was ready.

As the mighty forces approached the city, they were greeted by sounds of a festival in progress. Dismayed by the inhabitants' apparent lack of fear, the kings conferred and determined to cut off the water supply. Mahosadha responded by causing huge fountains to be built, and water flowed out of the city in prodigious quantities. Realizing that Mithila must have deep wells and vast stores of water, the kings next attempted to starve the city into submission. Whereupon Mahosadha had huge amounts of food dropped over the walls, saying that Mithila had more than it could use. Perhaps the enemy army might be hungry. The hundred and one kings were astonished. They determined to stop all fuel from entering the city, but once again they had no success. Mahosadha caused great pyres of wood to be burned in the moats surrounding the walls, demonstrating that he had an enormous surplus of fuel.

The kings redoubled their efforts to take the city, but to no avail. Mahosadha, watching from the ramparts of Mithila, anticipated their every effort to gain access to the city. Finally, near despair, Kevatta thought of a last ruse: "We shall meet outside the gates," he proposed, "and Mahosadha will have to salute me, for

I am by far the elder. We know that whoever does obeisance is conquered. This is one contest he cannot win."

Mahosadha instantly realized the implications of this challenge and devised a trick which would thwart the wicked Kevatta once again. Having learned from his spies of Kevatta's surpassing greed, Mahosadha advanced outside the city gates carrying an octagonal gem which glittered enticingly in the sunlight. Pretending to offer it to his enemy, Mahosadha dropped the jewel into the dirt. Kevatta immediately lunged to retrieve it. As he knelt on the ground, Mahosadha held Kevatta's shoulder blades with one hand and his back with the other so that the grasping sage could not stand up. Holding him thus, Mahosadha shouted loudly, "Rise, teacher, rise! I am younger than you, young enough to be your grandson. Do you no obeisance to me!"

Hearing these words, the hundred and one kings and their armies became frightened. If Kevatta had made obeisance to Mahosadha, then they were indeed lost. Without stopping even to retrieve their weapons, they fled.

Furious at his humiliation, Kevatta withdrew to the city of his king, Culani, in order to devise a new plan for defeating Mahosadha and King Vedeha. Finally he perfected a scheme for luring the king into his power. King Culani had a beautiful daughter. Her portrait, along with poems describing her beauty, was sent to Mithila and presented to the gullible King Vedeha. Soon befuddled with passion, King Vedeha determined to have her for his bride. Despite Mahosadha's warnings of trickery, Vedeha stubbornly persisted in his foolishness and began to plan his journey to Culani's kingdom.

At last Mahosadha decided that he would have to save the king in spite of himself. Obtaining permission to go to Culani's city four months in advance of Vedeha, he immediately set about outwitting Kevatta and King Culani. With his architectural genius, he proceeded to construct a splendid palace for King Vedeha on the outskirts of Culani's capital. This was no ordinary palace, for within it was the entrance to an underground tunnel filled with marvels never before seen by man. Embellished like a hall of the gods, its walls were covered with rich paintings and tapestries. Hanging lamps illuminated the passages, which were divided by eighty great doors and sixty-four small, all opening and closing at the touch of a finger. These led into a hundred and one bedchambers, similarly adorned and decorated with statues of beautiful women. The marvelous tunnel led to the royal palace where Culani's daughter lived and ended in a cave on the mouth of the Ganges river, some distance outside the city walls.

When all was ready, King Vedeha arrived at Culani's city, only to discover that he was in danger of his life. Waiting inside his new palace to receive his bride, he became aware of ominous numbers of Culani's troops gathering outside. At first he only questioned his four old sages, for he was ashamed to ask Mahosadha's advice after disregarding him completely. Each sage in turn shook his head in dismay and counseled suicide as the only alternative to slow death at the hands of the enemy. Finally Vedeha turned to Mahosadha and frantically begged for his help. For a time Mahosadha demurred, pretending that he was powerless, for he wished to impress the king's folly upon him. At last he revealed the tunnel, and Vedeha and his retinue escaped through its corridors.

Meanwhile, Mahosadha's soldiers crept through the tunnel in the direction of Culani's palace. Reaching the inner chambers of the palace, they pretended to be forces loyal to Culani. Extolling the riches of the marvelous tunnel, they persuaded the princess and her attendants to enter. They passed along the corridor and through the opulent chambers, each more sumptuous than the last. Finally they arrived at the cave, where they encountered King Vedeha and his retinue.

PLATE 12 *(facing page).* THE MAHOSADHA JATAKA *(Wat Bang Yi Khan, Thonburi): King Vedeha Laments While His Four Sages Confer.*

King Vedeha laments the attack on his kingdom, while his four sages appear at a loss as to what to advise. The palace consists of a walled-in courtyard, a facadeless interior with a solid red background, a jagged-edged screen behind the four sages, and the king's throne beneath the central spire of the rooftops. Trees and bushes seem to grow from the palace itself. Both the sages with their white, pointed caps and their mournful expressions and the commoners in their awkward efforts to stave off the attackers add humor to this scene.

PLATE 13 *(page 58).* THE MAHOSADHA JATAKA *(Wat Bang Yi Khan, Thonburi): One Hundred and One Kings on Their Way to Attack the Kingdom of Mithila.*

The multitude of Indian kings is here represented by the two figures on elephants. They and their soldiers, many of whom are foreign mercenaries on foot, are proceeding to the kingdom of Mithila. The procession, distinguished by bright colors and gold-leaf highlights, fits into a beautiful pattern of blunt-edged rocks and other landscape details of more subdued hues. King Culani, the expedition's leader, is seated proudly on the gray elephant. Stippling and shading, so rarely used in Thai painting, may be seen along the trunk, throat, jaw, eyelid, ear, and belly of the elephant.

For further comments, see page 137.

Although at first alarmed, the princess soon became reconciled to her abduction. She and King Vedeha were married, and with their entourage hastened back to Mithila by barge and fast elephant. In Culani's palace, the soldiers stole its treasures and strung up the dwarfs and hunchbacks who guarded the interior.

Mahosadha returned to the palace he had built and waited for Culani to discover the trick. Soon Culani learned of the disappearance of his family along with King Vedeha and sought out Mahosadha. He was astounded when he was escorted through the tunnel and shown its marvels. At length they reached the mouth of the cave. Suddenly Mahosadha brandished a sword at him, leaped fourteen cubits into the air, and shouted, "Whose are the kingdoms of India?"

PLATE 14 (*page 59*). THE MAHOSADHA JATAKA (*Wat Bang Yi Khan, Thonburi*): *Mahosadha Confronts the Hundred and One Kings of India.*

Mahosadha confronts the attacking kings of India, led by King Culani, who points to the ramparts where the defender Mahosadha stands calmly, one hand raised and the other holding a monk's fan. The protagonists, nicely highlighted in gold leaf, are seen from eye level, while the scene within the courtyard is seen from an aerial perspective.

PLATE 15 (*facing page, top*). THE MAHOSADHA JATAKA (*Wat Suwannaram, Thonburi*): *King Vedeha and Allies of Mahosadha.*

The scene framed within a doorway could be from a Mughal miniature. There is individualization in the facial features of the figures and in such details as turbans, long hair, potbellies, and costumes. King Vedeha is identified by his regal horse and pointing arm, not by any resemblance to the normal rendition of a king.

For further comments, see page 137.

PLATE 16 (*facing page, bottom*). THE MAHOSADHA JATAKA (*Wat Suwannaram, Thonburi*): *Kevatta Kneels to Retrieve Mahosadha's Jewel.*

Mahosadha holds the wicked Kevatta down as he bends to retrieve the jewel Mahosadha has dropped in order to trick him. The jewel is just far enough behind Mahosadha to force Kevatta to appear to kiss the sage's pointed slippers before reaching it, causing Kevatta's followers to look worried and flee. The victors, behind Mahosadha, remain calm; one of them even stifles a laugh. This is the scene used in the Traibhumi manuscript to illustrate this Jataka, with many of the same details. The picture space is cluttered, giving the impression of chaos.

Too frightened to speak, Culani cowered on his knees in mute defeat. Mahosadha then laid aside his sword, and the two swore a sincere friendship. The wicked Kevatta was banished and heard of no more. Thus did Mahosadha the Great Being bring a lasting peace to the kingdoms of India.

VI. BHURIDATTA THE NAGA PRINCE

(Illustrated on pages 65–66)

IN THE HIDDEN DEPTHS of the earth, far below the fields and woodlands of the world of men, dwell the nagas. They are magical serpents who can assume human form when they wish. Their kingdom glitters with rare jewels and precious minerals; they live in great splendor and richness. From time to time, they leave their realm and mingle with the human beings who inhabit the surface of the earth.

The archenemy of the naga is the garuda, the great bird who lives in the sunlit and airy skies. Once when a garuda was hungry he captured a naga and flew off with him. As he swept over the Himavat forest, clutching the head of the great snake in his claws, the naga was able to coil himself around a tall banyan tree. But the strength of the garuda was such that the tree was torn from its roots as he flew on.

After he had devoured the naga, the garuda remembered that the banyan tree had sheltered the hut of a hermit, and he feared that his unwitting deed might bring misfortune upon himself. He returned to the hermit's hut to ask him and was assured that he would suffer no ill on this account, for his action was not intended to harm. Pleased by this answer, the garuda rewarded the hermit by telling him the words of a magic snake charm of great power and gave him a fan behind which to chant it.

But as the hermit had no reason to use the charm, he gave it away to a Brahmin snake charmer named Alambayana who had been his faithful servant. Alambayana decided to use the charm to capture a mighty naga, which would earn him fame and wealth. He left the service of the hermit and wandered through the forest until he reached the banks of the Yamuna River. There he encountered a band of naga youths who had with them the precious jewel of the nagas, the "jewel that grants all desires.'' As soon as they heard the Brahmin muttering the magic spell of the garuda, they trembled with fear and sank into the water, leaving the glittering gem behind. Alambayana, delighted with his good fortune, picked up the jewel, though unaware of its magic powers, and continued into the forest.

A little later, he met a hunter and his son who earned their livelihood by capturing wild animals in the forest. When the hunter spied the jewel in the hand of Alambayana, he recognized it and was filled with greed and regret, for once before he had had the opportunity to possess the gem but had not taken it. He thought back to that time many years before and recalled how he had heard the music and laughter of naga maidens at dawn one morning after he had spent a night in the forest. When he had crept close to discover the cause of the merriment, the maidens had spied him and fled, leaving behind a princely snake dressed

PLATE 17 *(facing page, top).* THE BHURIDATTA JATAKA *(Wat Bang Yi Khan, Thonburi): The Garuda Talks with the Hermit.*

The garuda, regretful of having pulled up a banyan tree that had shaded a hermit's hut, goes to ask him if any harm will befall the garuda as a result. The hermit, judging from his unusual turban-like headgear and vials, fruits, and beads, is not an ordinary ascetic. A banner above his roof seems to have an eye drawn upon it; perhaps this man is a guru with visionary powers. The peculiar set of his hut also leads to speculation. Does it have rooms within rooms? Does it continue into a cave under the cliff? Who is entering the other hut? Is it the same hermit or Alambayana, his helper? The garuda, hands joined reverently, has a pointed beak and ears, human upper body, wings, lionlike legs and paws, and a kranok-shaped tail.

For further comments, see page 136.

PLATE 18 *(facing page, bottom).* THE BHURIDATTA JATAKA *(Wat No, Suphanburi): a) Alambayana Captures the Naga Prince b) Alambayana Stuffs Bhuridatta into a Basket.*

Alambayana, armed with his magical fan, grabs Bhuridatta by the tail and charms him off the high narrow anthill where he has been meditating. Naga maidens playing stringed instruments, who were to escort the prince back to the naga kingdom, flee at the sight of the snake charmer. They turn their heads back in time to glimpse the scene in which Bhuridatta is being crushed into Alambayana's basket. The inscription says: "This is when Alambayana captures the Bodhisatta; naga maidens have come to greet Bhuridatta with singing."

For further comments, see page 136.

in rich attire and coiled about a huge abandoned anthill. When the woodsman had approached him and asked who he might be, the prince had told him that he was Bhuridatta, prince of the nagas. He had earned the name Bhuridatta, or godly Datta, because of his wisdom and goodness. He had determined to increase his store of merit by leaving his wives and palace to live as an ascetic. He had found this abandoned anthill in the world of men, and every night he coiled his great length around it and remained there motionless until morning, vowing, "Let him who will take my skin or muscles or bones or blood." At dawn, he had explained, ten naga maiden attendants would come to escort him back to the realm of the nagas.

Bhuridatta did not want anyone to know about his place of meditation. To keep the woodsman from revealing it, he had invited him and his son to return with him to the naga kingdom and dwell in splendor there. They had accepted and in the realm of the nagas had lived in great ease and luxury. However, after a year of such a life, the hunter had become restless and longed to return to the world of men. Bhuridatta, anxious for him to stay, had offered him great riches, even to the very same "jewel that grants all desires," but the woodsman had refused them, saying that he wished to become an ascetic like Bhuridatta. Thus he and his son had returned to their former dwelling. When his wife learned, however, that he had decided to become a hermit and leave her again, she angrily told him that he must stay and help her support their family. So he had resumed his former life, a humble hunter as before.

Now when he saw the magic jewel in the hand of the Brahmin Alambayana, he regretted not having accepted it when Bhuridatta had offered it to him and determined to have it. First he tried to persuade Alambayana that the gem was dangerous, but the wily Brahmin could not be convinced to part with it. Then Alambayana spoke of the purpose of his wanderings: to find and capture a mighty

PLATE 19 (*facing page*). THE BHURIDATTA JATAKA (*Wat Yai Intharam, Chonburi*): *Bhuridatta Performs at the Court of the King of Benares.*

Alambayana is forcing the naga prince to dance before the king of Benares, who is seated on a dais at the right of the scene. The hermit in the center is Bhuridatta's brother disguised. In his hand he holds his sister in the shape of a frog with venom powerful enough to blow up the city. The king points an accusing finger at the wicked snake charmer who is to blame for this dangerous situation. The crowd at the left appears anxious and afraid.

For further comments, see page 136.

naga, which would win him fame and fortune. To anyone who could inform him of the whereabouts of such a snake he would give the glittering gem, whose powers he still did not realize.

The hunter saw in a flash how he could regain the wealth he had once given up. When he was about to tell Alambayana where the naga prince was hidden, his son tried to dissuade him from betraying his friend, who had trusted him to keep his secret and who had welcomed the hunter to his palace for a year. He urged his father to ask the naga prince himself for whatever riches he wanted, for he was certain that the naga would grant them.

But the greedy woodsman would not listen to his son's wise counsel and led Alambayana through the forest to the great anthill around which Bhuridatta was coiled. Anxious to capture the great serpent, Alambayana hastily handed the hunter his reward, the magic jewel. But as the hunter grabbed it eagerly, it slipped through his fingers and disappeared through a crack in the earth, to be reclaimed by the naga world whence it came. The foolish woodsman departed, lamenting his misfortune.

Alambayana, intent upon his evil deed, approached Bhuridatta, chanting the magic spell and waving the fan, and captured him with ease. The Bodhisatta, for such was Bhuridatta, submitted, obeying the precept he had set for himself: "Let him who will take my skin or muscles or bones or blood." Alambayana then crushed his bones and forced him into a basket. Although the naga prince suffered great pain, he permitted himself to feel no anger toward the Brahmin.

Alambayana took his prisoner to a nearby village and ordered him to perform. Unaffected by his cruel treatment, the great snake danced, assuming various colors and forms, spitting forth water and smoke, and causing great wonder among the villagers. The Brahmin profited greatly from Bhuridatta's astonishing talents, for the people gave him much money to see the snake perform. He went from village to village, amassing great wealth and renown, until at last he reached Benares.

Meanwhile, the wives and mother of Bhuridatta had missed him and sent his brothers to seek him. One brother went to search in the kingdom of the gods, one looked in the Himavat forest, and the eldest, Sudassana, searched in the world of men. Dressed as an ascetic, he was accompanied by Bhuridatta's favorite sister, who had disguised herself as a frog hidden in Sudassana's matted hair.

He searched the world of men in vain until finally he came to the city of Benares, where his mother's brother was now king. He arrived just as the people were gathering in the marketplace to watch the great snake perform. Bhuridatta lifted his head out of his basket and saw his brother in the crowd. He went to him, and placing his head on his brother's foot, he wept, and Sudassana wept also. Alambayana, seeing this from a distance, wondered if the snake had bitten the ascetic and assured Sudassana that his snake was not poisonous.

Sudassana answered proudly that no venom from a snake or any other creature could harm him. This retort made Alambayana angry and he challenged Sudassana to show his powers. The ascetic called forth his sister, who, in her form as a frog, contained a most poisonous venom. He asked her to spit three drops of her poison into his hand. Then he threatened Alambayana with these words: "Who sees these drops of poison waiting in my palm? Once they touch the ground, they have the power to blow up all of this city of Benares. Shall I show you?"

Alambayana shrank back, and the people cried out in fear. Only the king remained calm. He asked, "How can this poison be destroyed?"

Sudassana told him that the only way was to dig three enormous pits and to fill one with drugs, one with cow dung, and one with medicine. When this was done, he threw the three drops of poison into the three holes. They immediately exploded, filling the air with heat and thunder. The terrified Alambayana became as white as a leper, and he said three times, "I will set the naga prince free."

Whereupon Bhuridatta emerged from the jeweled basket and, assuming a radiant form, stood before the multitude in all his glory. The evil Brahmin crept away and was not seen again. The two brothers revealed themselves to the king as his nephews, and there was a great celebration before they returned to the naga kingdom.

At the end of his life, Bhuridatta, having succeeded in keeping the precepts, ascended to heaven with the hosts of virtuous nagas.

VII. CANDA-KUMARA THE HONORABLE PRINCE

(Illustrated on pages 73–74)

IN THE KINGDOM of Pupphavati near Benares, good Prince Canda-Kumara served his father, King Ekaraja, as viceroy, and became known throughout the realm for his patience and fairness in solving disputes. In those days, the chief court Brahmin, named Khandahala, had the ear of the king in all matters, both spiritual and temporal. This was unfortunate for the kingdom in general and Prince Canda in particular, because Khandahala was an unprincipled priest. An agent for the forces of evil, he had contrived to be appointed a judge, though he was in no way fair or honest, and was bent on destroying Prince Canda. The prince was the Brahmin's natural foe, for Canda was in fact the Bodhisatta and supported the powers of good in the world.

Now, it happened one day that Prince Canda was able to reverse a judgment that Khandahala had made in one case, and thereby restored some unjustly seized properties to their rightful owners. The news of this good deed spread to the people and they began to sing the praises of Prince Canda. They called on him continually to act as their mediator, and eventually the king conferred upon his son the office of judge.

Khandahala grew more and more jealous of Prince Canda. He plotted innumerable ways to get rid of the young prince who had replaced him in the people's affections. He planned a revenge that he thought would encompass the prince as well as the whole community, which had ceased to pay attention to him. Before long, he was able to put his scheme into execution.

One night, King Ekaraja dreamed of a glorious bejeweled heaven populated by celestial beings. When he awoke, he was seized by an overpowering desire to enter this radiant world. Having little religious insight himself, he went out onto the porch of his royal hall and bade his chief Brahmin to come to him. Still dazzled by his vision, he asked Khandahala to tell him the way to this resplendent abode.

Khandahala saw that this was his moment for revenge. As he knelt before the king, he said, "It will not be easy for you to find this realm, and it will cost you dearly. You must offer a splendid sacrifice to the gods. It must be made in units of four; only such a gift can win the attention of those on high. Sons, queens, merchants, beasts, these four kinds, sacrificed with proper ritual, will gain you entrance into this heaven."

So greatly had the king's dream affected him that he was no longer sound of mind. As a result he succumbed to Khandahala's dreadful advice. He gave orders straightaway to prepare for a massive sacrifice outside the city walls.

But Prince Canda soon divined the evil Brahmin's motives and grieved that so many should have to lose their lives on his account. He asked his father to forgo the sacrifice, not to save himself, for he was willing to die, but for the sake of the innocent victims.

A great sadness hung over the city, and one by one those close to King Ekaraja came and told him that the Brahmin spoke falsely. His aged parents pleaded with him to put an end to the plans for this bloody ordeal. But the power of the Brahmin was such that the king paid no heed. His ministers, his son's wife, and even his little grandson begged that this appalling sacrifice not be carried out. Each time the king appeared to falter in his resolve, Khandahala rushed in to remind him that this was the only way to heaven. Wailing filled the city. Once the king weakened and released the hapless victims, only to call them back into custody under renewed pressure from the evil priest.

At last all was in readiness: the ground was cleared and a platform raised; the pyre was draped, and the banners were hung. Multi-tiered umbrellas marked the significance of the place. Horses and bulls, unaware of impending death, strained and snorted at their stakes, impatient for release. Canda sat apart from his fellow

PLATE 20 *(facing page)*. THE CANDA-KUMARA JATAKA *(Wat Chang Yai, Ayuthaya)*: *Prince Canda Mourns the Loss of So Many Innocent Victims.*

Prince Canda laments not for himself but for the innocent ones who are to be sacrificed on his account as part of Khandahala's scheme. The figures in this panel have particularly long-bodied torsos; buildings are placed at uneven angles to one another against solid colors of subdued hues.

For further comments, see page 138.

victims, but all awaited the same fate. Amid the company of the mourners assembled was Prince Canda's wife. Realizing that the king would forever be deaf to her appeals, she called upon the gods. Clasping her hands as she walked, she beseeched the gods to heed her. "We on earth," she said, "can do no more. It is clear that even the spirits here are blind to justice or else in league with falsity and guile. I therefore raise my plea to you on high to end this sacrifice forthwith before the innocent fall dead on these defiled grounds."

Suddenly, like a thunderbolt, mighty Sakka appeared overhead. Surrounded by a flaming aureole, he brandished a mallet and chisel with which he struck at the royal umbrellas. As they fell under the blows the sacrifice was terminated, for without the umbrellas the ceremony was no longer sacred. At this amazing sight the crowd broke into joyous tumult, while the victims danced in a wild frenzy. The animals whinnied and roared in fright and broke their chains. People were crushed beneath the stampeding herd. The king swiftly mounted his elephant but had no place to turn. The crowd set upon the evil Brahmin and beat him to death. They would have killed the king as well, if Sakka had not restrained them for the sake of Prince Canda. He was, however, sent into exile and made to live as an outcast, though his son never forgot him and saw to his needs.

Gods and goddesses joined the people in the great festive occasion that was Prince Canda's coronation. As king, he continued to be just and self-restrained, and his reign was long and peaceful, ever worthy of a future Buddha.

PLATE 21 (*facing page*). THE CANDA-KUMARA JATAKA (*Wat Choeng Tha, Ayuthaya*): *Sakka Breaks the Sacrificial Umbrella and Ends the Evil Ceremony.*

Sakka, here framed by a tree instead of a halo, strikes down the ceremonial umbrellas with his mallet, while the sacrificial victims, seated on a platform, lament. Bulls rear up and stampede as their liberation approaches. The mob of villagers to the right grab the white-robed evil Brahmin by the feet and waist to kill him, while others run toward the pavilion of the king, to the right, to do away with him too for having heeded Khandahala's advice.

For further comments, see page 137.

VIII. NARADA THE GREAT BRAHMA

(Illustrated on pages 79–80)

IN THE KINGDOM of Videha, there lived King Angati and his beautiful daughter, Ruja. Ruja was his greatest joy, for though he had sixteen thousand wives, she was his only child. Upon her he lavished his wealth, sending her baskets of flowers, delicate trinkets, and garments of spun gold and silver. He even entrusted to her the honor of distributing every two weeks a thousand pieces of gold to the poor and sickly. This almsgiving won him the love of his people and the admiration of his daughter.

On the eve of the great festival of the full moon, King Angati, freshly bathed and dressed, stood with his three chief advisers surveying from his terrace the white city beneath him. As the streets gleamed with the rays of the advancing moon, the king turned to his counselors and asked, "How best shall we amuse ourselves on this festival eve?"

The first one, General Alata, suggested conquering new lands. The second, who was in charge of the king's diversions, thought only of feasting and dancing. The third, the chief court Brahmin, knew of a naked ascetic living in the forest just outside the city and felt that it would be most entertaining to go seek out his advice. Since King Angati had always enjoyed listening to ascetics, he agreed to the Brahmin's suggestion.

Thus the royal chariot, made of solid ivory, was polished and covered with silver ornaments for the king's nocturnal journey. White were the four swift horses that drew it, white was the seven-tiered umbrella, white the royal fan; from a distance, the king in his shining chariot could have been a shaft of moonlight.

As he and his entourage approached the center of the forest, they saw a crowd surrounding a naked man seated on the ground and knew this must be Guna the

77

ascetic. Not wanting to disturb the gathering, the king alighted from the chariot and greeted Guna on foot. After exchanging respectful words with him, King Angati seated himself at one side on a small mat covered with squirrel skins and told Guna the purpose of his visit. "The festival of the full moon is upon us," he said, "and we have come to ask you to remove some doubts from our minds."

He then proceeded to ask him the rules of right behavior toward parents and teachers, wives and children, Brahmins and the aged, the army and his people, adding, "And most important, we should like to know how it is that some men go to hell while others find their way to heaven."

Now, it happened that at that time and in that land there was no true sage to whom men could turn for advice, and by default Guna, though merely an ignorant mendicant, childish and given to half-truths, had gained a reputation for wisdom. Thus when Guna seized this occasion to recite his heretical theories, many people believed him. He spoke in this way: "There is no right or wrong way to behave. Whatever you do, whether it be virtuous or evil, has no effect on your future, for your life is arranged in advance of your birth. Whether a man thrusts his sword into his enemy's heart or whether he gives alms is irrelevant to a life over which we have no control. Hell? Heaven? Nonsense! There is no other world than this. So follow your own will and seek your own pleasure."

After Guna had finished his shocking speech, General Alata was the first to speak. "That confirms what I have always felt, for in a former birth I was a hunter, killing sacred cows and committing many wrongs. And yet do you see me suffer in this life? I am a prosperous general and have never been sent to hell."

Then a slave dressed in rags tearfully related how he had always been and still was a virtuous man, never failing to give alms in previous lives. "But look upon me now," he said, "a prostitute's son, with hardly enough to eat, and still I give half of my food away to those as hungry as I, and still I keep the fast days. But my past and present virtues go unheeded, alas!"

King Angati, swayed by the stories he heard, spoke of his own unfailing devo-

PLATE 22 (facing page). THE NARADA JATAKA (Wat Yai Intharam, Chonburi): Ruja Tells the People That She Has No Alms to Give Them.

From a pavilion decorated with curtains wrapped about columns, Ruja, leaning on one hand, her arm twisted back, tells the people who have come for alms why there are none. The men below have coarse facial features and a variety of skin colors. Visibly upset by the news, they display a range of emotions on their faces.

tion to almsgiving, but still he was not satisfied, saying, "Though I have not suffered as a result of my good deeds, I have not had a bit of enjoyment from them either." And convinced of the truth of Guna's words, he abruptly turned from the ascetic and, without saluting him, departed.

From then on, he resolved to make no further effort to do good. He relinquished all cares and unpleasant kingly duties to his advisers. He no longer made decisions. He busied himself only with watching others at work and at play. Since nothing he did was to have any consequences, he reasoned, he would have no more to do with the business of life. Worst of all, he stopped giving alms.

A month passed, and his subjects lamented the loss of their king's interest in them. Ruja wept for her father, for she heard the mourning of his unhappy people and saw him harden his heart and close his ears to reason.

On the next festival of the full moon, Ruja dressed herself in her finest garments, gifts from her father, and entered his court. When he inquired how she was enjoying life, she answered that she lacked only one thing. She explained: "Tomorrow, my father, is the sacred fifteenth day. Please order, if you will, your courtiers to bring me a thousand pieces of gold that I may bestow them at once upon the people, as has been your custom."

Her father replied indifferently, "Alms? Give away our gold? I have no wish to carry on such a foolish custom; destiny makes us what we are. For what reason should I waste my wealth? Please do not annoy me further with such inconsequential matters, my daughter."

Ruja realized with horror that her father had truly strayed from the holy precepts. She pleaded with him thus: "O my father, I have heard that he who listens to fools himself becomes a fool and that he who lets himself be led by children himself becomes a child. I fear that Guna's words have turned you into such a one. As for your prosperous General Alata, he is merely reaping the good from past acts of merit, but it will soon be used up and he will go straight to hell. The beggar who ranted to you of his sufferings must be making up for some grave

PLATE 23 *(facing page)*. THE NARADA JATAKA *(Wat Yai Intharam, Chonburi): The Bodhisatta Narada Descends from Brahma Heaven.*

Narada descends in answer to Ruja's call; his enclosure in a flame-outlined halo detaches him from normal limits of time and space. But his halo overlaps the palace wall, placing him in contact with earth. Ruja's arms are raised high above the wall in reverence to him. The courtyard, seen as if from above, is enclosed by a zigzag wall.

misdemeanor in his past and will soon come to the end of his misery. The good he is doing now, along with his accumulated merit, will bring him to know the joys of heaven."

Then Ruja related how she herself, seven births ago, was born as a blacksmith's son who, with his wicked friends, used to corrupt other men's wives. As a result, in succeeding lives Ruja had been born as a castrated goat, a monkey whose father had cruelly removed his son's testicles, a eunuch, and other mutilated beings. Though the king still loved his daughter, he was unmoved by her arguments and refused to budge from his fixed opinions.

Ruja then stepped to one side of the court, knelt down, and with her hands together above her head, made reverences in ten directions to the highest deities, those in the Brahma heavens, begging them to give some sign which would shock her father out of his heresy.

At that moment the Bodhisatta, whose name was Narada and who was the Great Brahma of that time, was looking earthward from his seat in his heaven. He happened to hear Ruja's supplications and decided to help her. Before taking the journey to earth, he thought to himself, "There is none other than I who can drive away false doctrines. I shall go to the king in some unusual garb so that first my appearance and then my words will arrest his attention. King Angati values ascetics. I will dress like the most striking of them, and when he sees me, he will listen well."

The four-faced Great Brahma dressed according to his word, in a red-mottled garment with a black antelope skin over one shoulder. He carried a golden pole on his shoulders from which two golden begging bowls were suspended by strings of pearls. His hair was matted as is the custom of ascetics, but with a golden needle tucked inside. Thus arrayed, he sped through the sky like the moon when the clouds race past it on a windy night, and stood suspended in the air before the king and his court.

Ruja, who had returned to the king's side, immediately recognized the Brahma and bowed down to pay reverence to him. But the king, alarmed by the heavenly presence, rushed down from his throne to cry, "Who are you? From where do you come?"

Narada answered in this solemn way: "I am the Great Brahma from the Brahma heavens. I have come to tell you, King Angati, that you are condemning yourself to hell."

"I say there is no heaven or hell," Angati boasted. "To prove it, lend me five hundred pieces of gold, and if I am wrong, I will return one thousand pieces to you from hell when I am there."

Narada warned him in this way: "If you were a virtuous man, I would gladly lend you gold, for it is not hard to collect a debt from a man in heaven. But men like you, denying the precepts, following false doctrines, are bound for hell, and when you hear what I will tell you about hell, you will see that no one would dare collect a debt from a man in such a place. There is not just one hell, but a thousand hells. Animals of all sizes will chew on your skin and bite at your bones. Flocks of ravens, crows, and vultures will prey upon you. Dogs with iron teeth will tear at your entrails. Hot winds, razor-edged mountains, burning coals, and sword-leafed trees will torture you."

At last Angati was moved and trembled with fear. He looked to the Bodhisatta for help and asked him humbly how he could uncloud his mind and regain his senses. Narada then told him that while he was king and in good health, he should assume the responsibilities of his realm, providing for the poor, the hungry, the aged, and the Brahmins. "Let your mind guide your body, making you a sure but self-restrained man," he said. "Only then will you find the path to heaven. Let your daughter teach you, for she has learned the right way."

King Angati begged forgiveness and, with his daughter, bowed in reverence and gratitude to the Bodhisatta, who then turned and sped back to the Brahma world.

IX. VIDHURA-PANDITA
THE ELOQUENT SAGE

(Illustrated on pages 87–88)

A T ONE TIME, thousands of years ago, the Bodhisatta came to earth in the person of a sage named Vidhura-Pandita. He was no ordinary man of wisdom. His life's purpose was to speak the truth, and in such a way that men would be held spellbound by his voice. As chief counselor to the righteous King Dhananjaya in the city of Indapatta, Vidhura fulfilled his mission well. His eloquent tongue had such power that one hundred and one kings from faraway lands, hypnotized by the sage's sweet voice, were unable to return to their kingdoms.

He was known throughout many worlds. A naga queen, after hearing her husband describe the incomparable sage, longed to hear him speak. But it would have been unseemly for her, a mere female, to ask her husband to bring Vidhura to her. Instead, she feigned illness and took to her sickbed, moaning aloud that only one thing could cure her: the heart of Vidhura. "O King, O Monarch of the Nagas," she cried. "Bring me Vidhura's heart or I shall die!"

The king was so distraught that his face became instantly old and withered, like a lotus touched by human hands. How could such a feat be accomplished? Who would have the mind and heart to carry out such a low deed? For though the king wished to save the life of his queen, he also knew the peerless qualities of the sage and mourned the need to command such an act. At that moment he caught sight of his beautiful daughter, Princess Irandati, and resolved to send her out to seek a husband who could wrest the heart from Vidhura.

The princess went off to the Himalayas to gather fragrant flowers of all colors. She adorned herself with them and made a bed of the most beautiful ones. She then began a seductive dance and sang, "What god or human, what gandhabba or sage, what naga or yakkha, able to make all wishes come true, will marry me this very night?"

85

At that time a yakkha, or demon, named Punnaka was riding on his magic horse over the Black Mountain. Hearing Irandati's love call, he stopped short, listened, and changed his course to ride over to her. Completely enamored, he resolved to marry her. Together they rode to the palace to ask her father's permission to be joined in wedlock. The king secretly rejoiced that his plan was bearing fruit, but to Punnaka he sternly announced that he would agree to the marriage only on one condition: that Punnaka first obtain the flesh of the heart of Vidhura. Pleased at the chance to prove his magical powers, Punnaka readily accepted the offer.

His hair trimmed, his horse sparkling with jewels from ear to hoof, Punnaka, sumptuously dressed, rode off into the sky to Indapatta, the kingdom where Vidhura dwelled. Before he reached the city, he made up his mind to win the sage as his prize in a game of dice to which he would challenge King Dhananjaya. Once inside the city's gates he said, "O mighty king, accept a game of dice with

PLATE 24 (*facing page, top*). THE VIDHURA-PANDITA JATAKA (*Wat Yai Intharam, Chonburi*): *The Dice Game Between King Dhananjaya and Punnaka.*

The dice game is played by King Dhananjaya and the yakkha Punnaka and witnessed by royal wives, nobles, and the goddess who is the king's guardian. As Punnaka holds the dice container, he stares at the king as if to end the king's luck. In other murals, he usually stares at the guardian deity. In either case, the goddess is frightened away; here she is hovering in the doorway, about to depart. Proportion varies here; the goddess appears smaller than the other characters, while the yakkha Punnaka appears slightly larger.

For further comments, see page 136.

PLATE 25 (*facing page, bottom*). THE VIDHURA-PANDITA JATAKA (*Wat Yai Intharam, Chonburi*): *a) Vidhura Takes Leave of His Family b) Vidhura Holds onto the Tail of Punnaka's Horse.*

Emphasis is placed on the scene of Vidhura hanging onto the tail of Punnaka's horse by enclosing the scene in a halo and placing it close to the center of the painting. Punnaka's position is the same as in the previous scene, in which Vidhura takes leave of his lamenting family. A transition is thereby effected between Vidhura's courtly life and his confrontation with evil forces, between life and possible death. By marking such a turning point, the artist has expressed psychological unity through composition. The Thai words on the wall behind the leavetaking scene read: "The story of the Lord Vidhura."

For further comments, see pages 134 and 138.

me, and if you win, a wondrous horse and magic gem will be yours." Whereupon he demonstrated the supernatural power of his horse to walk on water, stand on the palm of his hand, fly in the air, and gallop along the narrow city wall. The yakkha then commanded his precious lapis lazuli to perform miracles, to create living things, other worlds, the sun, the moon, and the constellations.

The king was so dazzled by Punnaka's magic possessions that he accepted the game, saying that should he lose, "Except my body and my white umbrella, all that I have shall be yours." That was just what Punnaka wanted to hear, for he knew that he would use his magic to turn his opponent's dice against him and win.

The hall was readied, a central platform was cleared, and other kings were called in as witnesses. The dice board was set up, and the two sat down to play. Punnaka insisted that the king have the first play. The dice were thrown. But something strange was happening. The king could see the falling dice turn against him by some magic power. Now, this perplexed him, because whenever he engaged in play, his guardian deity, his mother in a previous existence, was always there to see that he won. This time, however, she could do no more than hover in a doorway behind the king and warn him before the dice fell that they were about to go against him. Heeding her advice, the first time the dice were thrown he deftly caught them and threw them again. A second time they fell against him.

PLATE 26 (facing page). THE VIDHURA-PANDITA JATAKA (Wat Choeng Tha, Ayuthaya): a) Irandati Seduces Punnaka b) Vidhura Is Dragged Through the Sky by Punnaka's Magic Horse c) Punnaka Brings Vidhura to the Naga Kingdom.

These three forest scenes are drawn from the beginning, middle, and late parts of the story. In the first, Irandati is dancing and beckoning to Punnaka in an effort to seduce him; she is leading him to the sea below, where he will meet her father the naga king. The yakkha is still on horseback and riding vigorously toward her, emphasizing the eagerness of his response.

The second scene, under the first and below some trees, shows Vidhura, bent-legged, holding onto the tail of Punnaka's horse as it gallops through the sky, while the yakkha turns back and looks at his victim.

Above both of these scenes and to the right, Punnaka and Vidhura ride together on the magic horse in the direction of the sea, for Punnaka, having been converted by Vidhura, is going to transport him to the naga kingdom.

The scenes, all of which depict flying through the sky above rooftops, float against brown flat ground between rich green trees.

It became evident that the goddess could no longer help him, because Punnaka's magic was more powerful than hers.

Moreover, when Punnaka noticed that the king was aware of the way the dice were turning, he recognized the existence of an opposing force. All at once he spied the guardian goddess behind the king. To end her power, he glared at her with a murderous look in his angry eyes. Alarmed, the delicate deity fled from the pinnacled roof to the top of a nearby mountain. From then on, Punnaka's magic held sway, and the third time the king tossed the dice, he let them fall and lost. The yakkha then took his turn and won.

Punnaka, gleeful in victory, clapped his hands and called for his payment: the sage Vidhura. The king was jolted. "Vidhura? My most trusted counselor? My refuge and strength?"

Punnaka was unrelenting. "Are you the king's slave or his kinsman?" he rudely shouted at Vidhura, knowing well that Vidhura would answer in the most humble way. Vidhura agreed that he could be given away, and it was thus that he was delivered into the hands of the ill-intentioned yakkha.

But first, Vidhura asked Punnaka's permission to preach to his wives and sons. In keeping with his purpose on earth, he felt that he had to explain the principles of the doctrine before he could take leave of them. On the third day, he had completed what he had to say and calmly resigned himself to his unknown destiny. His wives, sons, servants, and friends all wept and prostrated themselves at his departure.

Punnaka looked upon his victim and declared, "You are about to cross from life to death; a long journey awaits you. Take hold of the tail of my magic steed; you shall not see again the world of men."

The Bodhisatta answered resolutely, "I fear no being, for I have harmed no one, in mind or in speech or in deed. Therefore naught can harm me." Where-upon he pulled his garments about him and gripped the horse's tail. In this way, they galloped across the sky to the Black Mountain. But contrary to Punnaka's hopes, neither the rocks nor the trees there so much as brushed Vidhura, and when they reached the peak, his victim was still alive.

Punnaka then tried to frighten Vidhura to death. He took on many shapes which would have made the most courageous of men swoon. Yet demons, lions, elephants, gigantic serpents, whirlwinds—all these terrifying forms failed to ruffle the calm of the Bodhisatta.

Punnaka, so expert at manipulating nature through trickery and disguise, realized that he could no longer resort to those means to kill his prisoner. He would have to use his own hand. In a flash, he seized the sage violently and, from where he stood at the summit of the mountain, whirled him around with his head downward facing the open expanse of the world. Dangling there, upside down to the earth, he, the embodiment of truth and wisdom, quietly addressed his executioner. "What is your reason for killing me?" When Punnaka told him why, the Bodhisatta immediately perceived that all concerned had misinterpreted the naga queen's request for his heart. She had not meant his physical heart. It was the heart of his wisdom that she desired. Vidhura was content, however, to say simply that if Punnaka would first listen to his teachings, he would then be willing to give up his heart to him.

Punnaka placed him on the ground, and at that moment a richly decorated throne appeared beneath the sage. Punnaka listened at Vidhura's feet, his hands joined in reverence. It was then that the giant became deeply conscious of his wrongdoing and was converted to the Right Way. He told his prisoner that he was a free man again.

Rather than return immediately to his kingdom, however, the Bodhisatta asked to be taken to the naga kingdom in order to resolve the misunderstanding. Together they rode on Punnaka's horse until the splendid naga palace came into sight, surrounded by the billowing sea and the strange creatures that inhabit it. Once inside the court, Vidhura was seated on the central throne, surrounded by the naga king and queen, their daughter Irandati, and Punnaka. From this place of honor, he offered his listeners his wisdom and his heart. He no longer cared for his life, for he had already given of his teachings. But the naga king, having discovered that the heart of a sage is his wisdom, no longer desired the flesh of Vidhura's heart. The naga queen, whose misunderstood words had led to this grave situation, dared not utter a word.

All questions resolved, the king gave his daughter to the yakkha in marriage and ordered him to return the sage to the court of his king. Once more Punnaka called for his magic steed and, carrying Vidhura in front and his bride behind, rode off into the sky toward Indapatta, the sage's home.

X. VESSANTARA THE CHARITABLE PRINCE

(Illustrated on pages 95–96 and 101–2)

THE TIME HAD COME for Phusati, Sakka's principal consort, to leave Tavatimsa heaven; on descending to earth, she became the mother of the Bodhisatta in his next-to-last birth.

In her rebirth in the world of men she was still called Phusati and grew into a most beautiful young girl. At the age of sixteen she was wed to Sanjaya, king of Sivi; they loved each other dearly. When she became aware that she was carrying a child, she had six alms halls built, from which she distributed silver daily. As the birth of her child grew imminent, she expressed the wish to visit every part of her husband's capital city. The king granted her request and had a lying-in shelter made ready to follow her. On approaching the Vessa, or merchant sector, her labor began. Behind the shelter she gave birth to a son. Having taken his first breath of air from the commercial quarter, the newborn child was named Vessantara, though he possessed none of the avarice of a merchant. For at that time a miracle occurred: the baby spoke to say, "Mother, what gift can I make?" causing the gods in heaven to take notice of this Great Being.

When he was eight years old, the boy expressed the desire to be able to give away something of his very own, something that had not been given him by another. He said, "If someone should ask me for my heart, I would give it to him, or my eye, or my flesh." This unusual wish attracted the attention of the gods, so that the earth quaked and thunder rumbled in the clouds over the Himavat.

As a youth, Vessantara contented himself with giving away readily and frequently the things he had acquired. At sixteen, his formal studies completed, the kingdom was given over to him and a marriage arranged between the king-to-be and Princess Maddi, daughter of a neighboring king. The kingdom prospered, and their marriage was happy. A son, Jali, and a daughter, Kanhajina, were born to them.

Years before, when Vessantara was a baby, a young white elephant had been brought to the royal stables. The two princely beings grew up together. It was on this white elephant that Vessantara visited his mother's alms halls six times a month to distribute gold. Indeed, many of his subjects attributed the prosperity of the kingdom and the benign rains that watered the fields to the virtue of the white elephant.

At this time the nearby kingdom of Kalinga was suffering from a prolonged drought. All the prayers of its people, all the supplications and offerings of its king were to no avail. Many in the kingdom had heard of the great white elephant and of Vessantara's generosity. They suggested that the king send eight Brahmin emissaries to ask Vessantara for the favored creature. The king agreed. When the Brahmins arrived at Sivi, King Vessantara was distributing alms from the elephant. The valuable beast was covered with precious gems and caparisoned with trappings of great worth. But on hearing their request, the king granted it immediately, pouring water into their hands to indicate the gift, so great was his desire to be charitable. When the gods saw this noble act, the earth shook and the skies were filled with thunder and lightning.

The citizens of Vessantara's kingdom were so distressed by the loss of the great animal that had brought them prosperity that they forced King Sanjaya to resume control of the kingdom and banish Vessantara. His parents were heartbroken, but

PLATE 27 (*facing page, top*). THE VESSANTARA JATAKA (*Wat Rachasitharam, Thonburi*): *Sakka Asks Phusati to Descend to Earth to Give Birth to Vessantara.*

Sakka, from a cushioned throne in Tavatimsa heaven, invites Phusati to be the future mother of the Bodhisatta Vessantara. Sakka, with one hand up to preach, sits at a level above Phusati, whose hands are joined in a gesture of reverence. Heaven is little more than a variation of the walled-in palace courtyard of an earthly king, with fruit-bearing trees of different sorts and celestial maiden attendants.

PLATE 28 (*facing page, bottom*). THE VESSANTARA JATAKA (*Wat Rachasitharam, Thonburi*): *Vessantara and Maddi on Foot Carrying Their Children.*

Having given away their chariot, Vessantara and Maddi continue their journey on foot, a child in each one's arms. Vessantara's strength is felt in his raised head, the casual slinging of his sword over one shoulder, and the way he stretches one leg forward.

the people's fury was so great that he was granted only one day's grace before exile. On that day Vessantara gave away all his possessions, seven hundred of each kind: elephants, horses, chariots, maidens, slaves, and many others. This was known as the Gift of the Seven Hundreds; people came from far away, each to receive a gift. Vessantara was still distributing them when night fell. Then, with his wife and children, who would not be left behind, he spent his last night taking leave of his parents.

The banished family left the city at sunrise in a chariot drawn by four horses. No sooner had the city gates closed behind them than they met four Brahmins. Having arrived too late for the Gift of the Seven Hundreds, the Brahmins now asked for the four horses, which were promptly granted them. The gods dispatched four deities in the form of stags to draw the chariot. However, shortly thereafter a fifth Brahmin appeared, asking for the chariot. Vessantara agreed gladly, the stags disappeared, and the noble prince and his wife continued on their way by foot, the boy in his father's arms, the girl in her mother's.

Their journey took them first to Ceta, a city ruled by Vessantara's uncle, where they rested for a day and a night in a hall beside the city gates, for they

PLATE 29 (facing page, top). THE VESSANTARA JATAKA (Wat Rachasitharam, Thonburi): A Hermit Shows Jujaka the Way to Vessantara's Hut.

The Brahmin Jujaka bends his bony body, giving the hermit a toothless grin and reverent greeting in gratitude for the directions given him. The hermit, dressed in typical ascetic's garments, reveals his age only in the folds of his neck and some lines on his face. He touches Jujaka in a gesture of friendliness as he talks to him. The plants, trees, and earth are particularly beautiful in this painting.

For further comments, see pages 134 and 136.

PLATE 30 (facing page, bottom). THE VESSANTARA JATAKA (Wat Rachasitharam, Thonburi): Maddi Is Detained by Wild Animals.

Before Maddi realizes that her children have been given away and are being mistreated by their owner, two tigers and a sing (mythical lion) are sent by the gods to detain her from returning to the hermitage and thus spare her suffering. The sing has swirls on his body and pointed kranok designs on his head, flanks, and shoulders resembling cock's combs or tufts of hair. His whole body is outlined by featherlets. The tigers' markings resemble those on Maddi's garments, which are made of tiger skin. The animals appear quite fierce, but Maddi kneels before them serenely, her hands joined in reverence.

were unwilling to enter the city, although the king had invited them to rule in his stead. When they left the city the king of Ceta accompanied them to the nearby forest, leaving them with a woodsman who guided them as far as the river. There they rested and were given food. They then set out alone into the foothills of the Himalayas, skirting the shores of the great Mucalinda Lake, and at length they reached the mountains. A narrow path took them through a forest to the foot of Mount Vamka.

Sakka, the king of the gods, anticipating their arrival, had ordered his architect Vissakamma to construct two hermitages beside a lotus pond. Vessantara went ahead. On entering one of the buildings alone, he found four sets of ascetic's robes neatly folded and knew that Sakka was observing him. He dressed, took the vows of an ascetic, then went out to greet his wife Maddi. She and the children followed his example. They lived in separate huts by the pond for seven months, eating the roots and jungle fruits which Maddi collected each day. Although Maddi looked after her husband, they never so much as touched each other, for both had sworn chastity.

Meanwhile, in Kalinga the drought had broken with the arrival of the white elephant. In a village there, lived a poor Brahmin, Jujaka by name, who had a beautiful young wife. When she went to the well for water, she was frequently reviled and teased by the village women for caring so well for her old and ugly husband. At last she refused to go to the well any longer. She insisted that Jujaka find her some servants in order to spare her ridicule. Having heard of Vessantara's fabled generosity, she suggested that Jujaka seek him out and ask him for his two children to serve her.

As Jujaka was penniless and unable to buy slaves, he set out to find Vessantara. While passing through the forest near Ceta, he was attacked by watchdogs kept there by the king to prevent people from seeking out Vessantara. By saying that he had been sent by King Sanjaya to bring Vessantara back, Jujaka was able to trick the dogs' keeper, a huntsman, into letting him pass. He repeated the same story to a forest hermit, who reluctantly directed him to Vessantara's hermitage.

Jujaka waited until Maddi had departed into the forest the next morning before he approached the hermitage. As soon as Vessantara caught sight of the old man he was overjoyed, for he knew that at last he had an opportunity to make a supreme gift. As Jujaka made his unusual request, Vessantara agreed to give away his two beloved children. When the children overheard their exchange of words, they ran away to hide under the broad leaves of the lotus plants in the pond. Soon their father found them and called them back. He presented them to Jujaka by pouring water over his outstretched hands. The gods were disturbed, the earth quaked, and there was a great tumult in the heavens.

The Brahmin bound the children's hands with a jungle creeper, whipping them on their way. Tears streamed from Vessantara's eyes, and he went into his hut weeping. When he realized that the cause of his grief was his affection for his children, he set his mind on nonattachment and soon regained the calm of an ascetic.

As Jujaka drove the wailing children through the forest, the gods thought what anguish Maddi would suffer if she should see them thus. Three of the deities took the forms of a lion, a tiger, and a leopard that blocked the path of Maddi, thus preventing her return to the hermitage until after night had fallen. Vessantara could not bring himself to tell her what had become of the children. The distraught mother searched for them until dawn. When morning came, she returned to her hut and collapsed in a faint. Vessantara was in great distress. Breaking his ascetic's vows, he raised his wife up, then rubbed her face and bosom with water to revive her. When she was restored, he told her of his gift of the children. Understanding his desire to give away all he possessed, she did not protest. Instead, she rejoiced in his opportunity to make a supreme gift in his effort to achieve omniscience.

There remained one last and greatest gift, a devoted wife, and Sakka in his wisdom knew that Vessantara would not withhold it. To keep Vessantara from giving Maddi away to anyone else, Sakka assumed the guise of a Brahmin and approached the hermitage that same morning. Only then did Vessantara realize that he must also give away his dear wife to attain his goal. He gave her willingly to the old Brahmin, pouring water over his hands. Maddi submitted without a word, knowing that this would fulfill her husband's greatest wish: to have perfect knowledge. The heavens shook, the oceans roared, and the gods acknowledged that Vessantara had truly achieved omniscience. Then, having seen that the Great Being was capable of supreme charity, Sakka returned Maddi to him.

Meanwhile, Jujaka was lost in the forest. At night while he slept in the branches of a tree, he left the children bound to the trunk. However, deities took the shapes of their parents to nurture and protect them. The gods also guided the path of Jujaka so that although he intended to return to Kalinga, he and the children soon found themselves in Sivi. There the children were recognized and brought before King Sanjaya along with their captor. The king was so overjoyed at finding his grandchildren that he did not punish Jujaka. Instead, he paid the Brahmin a great ransom, with which the old man built himself a splendid mansion. There he lived sumptuously, but unaccustomed to such richness, he overate and died.

King Sanjaya questioned the children about their parents and was told that they were alive and well. But Jali reproached his grandfather for sending Vessantara away, accusing the king of not loving his son enough. Whereupon King Sanjaya determined to go to Mount Vamka in order to bring the royal couple back to Sivi.

To this end he ordered the road to be made smooth and wide, so that chariots could move along it. He ordered his generals thus: "Prepare my armies, elephants, horses, chariots, and banners, to make a royal procession to fetch my son back to Sivi. The road must be strung with garlands and offerings, with plenty of food and wine to assuage the hunger and thirst of the travelers. Let there be music and singing as we proceed."

When all was prepared, the great host set off for Mount Vamka, the king and Jali leading the way. They moved across the plains, into the forest, and around Mucalinda Lake, at last reaching the foot of the mountains.

All this while, Vessantara and Maddi had lived peacefully at the hermitage. As King Sanjaya's procession approached, Vessantara could hear the noise of marching armies, elephants, and chariots. At first he was alarmed, thinking that they were enemies come to take his life. He and Maddi climbed a nearby hill to survey the scene. Maddi, recognizing the banners as those of Sivi, reassured him, and they returned to the hermitage.

King Sanjaya approached them first and gravely inquired after their welfare. Assured of their well-being, he called his wife, Phusati, and the children to join them. So great was their joy at being reunited that all fell weeping on the ground in a faint. The gods took pity, the earth shook, lightning flashed in the clouds, and from the skies fell a shower of heavenly rain that revived the royal family. King Sanjaya asked Vessantara to return to rule the kingdom, for the people, regretting his departure, wished him to be their king once more.

Vessantara, having given all, was willing to resume his kingly role. He put away his hermit's robes. Three times he circled the hut, saying, "Here I have attained

PLATE 31 *(facing page).* THE VESSANTARA JATAKA *(Wat Rachasitharam, Thonburi): Sakka Descends to Ask for Maddi.*

Vessantara looks up at Sakka, realizing he will be asked to give away his most precious possession, his wife. The hermitage is a peculiar set of houses with Chinese-style curving rooftops, doorways inside doorways, and odd stone and geometrically designed surfaces.

omniscience,'' and prostrated himself before it. Then he was bathed, had his hair trimmed, and was dressed in princely garments, so that he shone with great splendor. Maddi was similarly arrayed in beautiful cloths and gems. Thus they proceeded to the camp of King Sanjaya.

After a month of joyful festivities in the forest, they returned to Sivi with great pomp. King Vessantara mounted the throne and by Sakka's will was endowed with treasures sufficient for distribution until the end of his life. After reigning gloriously for many years, the king passed away to Brahma's heaven, to remain a symbol of generosity for all time.

PLATE 32 *(facing page).* THE VESSANTARA JATAKA *(Wat Rachasitharam, Thonburi): King Sanjaya Leads a Royal Procession to Vessantara's Hermitage.*

While King Sanjaya leads the way on elephant-back, his queen and grandchildren follow in covered howdahs on two elephants (not shown). Attendants in lines walk ahead of and beside the king, some bearing umbrellas and standards, other wearing the dunce-cap crowns frequently seen in old Thai manuscript paintings. The procession flows along the lines of the rocks and trees.

For further comments, see pages 131 and 135.

BACKGROUND

THE JATAKA TALES

THE PRECISE ORIGINS of the Jataka tales are unknown, but some undoubtedly are derived from a very ancient stock of literature. Stories similar to certain Jatakas appear in the Old Testament and Aesop's fables, and later in the works of Chaucer, La Fontaine, and other Western writers; resemblances among the stories suggest that they may share a common Indo-European base.[1] Also, many Indian tales were carried to the West by mariners and other travelers, and were widely known in Europe in the Middle Ages.[2] From this same body of oral verse and legend evolved masterpieces of Indian literature, such as the great epic poem the *Mahabharata,* whose written form dates from the third or fourth century B.C.[3] In India in the sixth century B.C., when Gotama Buddha lived, these verses and tales had not been written down. The Jataka tales have survived in their present form because they were included in the teachings of the Buddha and eventually recorded.

THE LIFE OF THE BUDDHA   Like the tales, the account of the Buddha's life which has come down to us was transmitted orally for many centuries. The version known today is undoubtedly a mixture of fact and legend. It is believed by Theravada Buddhists that the Buddha was born in 624 B.C., although some scholars think that this date is too early and that it is more likely to have been about 543 B.C.[4] He was a member of the Kshatriya, or warrior, class, of the Sakya clan, and was called by the name Siddhattha, the family name being Gotama. His father ruled a small kingdom at Kapilavattu in what is now southernmost Nepal. At his birth a sage predicted that the child would become either a great ruler or a Buddha, an Enlightened One. In order to prevent Siddhattha from choosing the holy way, his father kept him sheltered from knowledge of the world outside the palace. At the age of sixteen he married a princess whom he won in a contest of arms and who later bore him a son. It was not until Siddhattha was twenty-nine that the sight of an old man, a sick man, a dead man, and an ascetic made him aware of the suffering which existence brings to all men. He decided to renounce the world and become an ascetic in order to understand the meaning of life.

For six years he practiced the utmost austerities, fasting almost to the point of starvation. Although he learned to control his mind, he did not reach Enlightenment. At last he decided that the Truth could not be found through extreme asceticism, and he accepted some food from a village maid. Having eaten and bathed, he sat beneath a pipal tree and meditated, determined to attain that indescribable state of complete tranquillity and knowledge which is Bodhi, or Enlightenment.

Mara, symbolic king of evil and temptation, mustered his forces in an effort to prevent the Buddha from achieving this perfect state. But the Buddha, putting his fingers to the ground, called on Dharani, the earth goddess, to bear witness to his right to Enlightenment through the accumulated virtue of many previous lives. Dharani did so by causing a flood that routed the armies of Mara. Having defeated the forces of evil, the Buddha continued to meditate until he reached Enlightenment, whereupon he perceived clearly the nature of existence. He then spent the rest of his life preaching the Dhamma, or doctrine of suffering and renunciation, until he died and passed into Nibbana.

The Buddha taught that life is unsatisfactory because of the transitory nature of all things and because of man's imperfections: greed, ill will, and self-delusion. A man could best overcome his faults by giving up his family and all material possessions except for a monk's robe and alms bowl. Having nothing, desiring nothing, he could devote his energies to meditation and study. Thus, many of the Buddha's followers were called to the monastic life, where they hoped to find the way to tranquillity, self-awareness, and perhaps eventually Nibbana, the end of existence and suffering.

EVOLUTION OF THE CANON   Although the Buddha lived and taught only in the region of northeastern India, after his death in 544 B.C. his teachings were taken to many parts of the land. In the third century B.C., Buddhism was given a great impetus by the conversion of Asoka, king of the Mauryas. After an especially bloody war with the kingdom of Kalinga, Asoka was filled with remorse at the horrors he had perpetrated and became a convert to the Dhamma. King Asoka made Buddhism the official religion of the kingdom and determined to make it a world religion as well. He sent missionaries all over India, to Ceylon, and as far as the Middle East, to Egypt and Syria.

As the years passed, the followers of the Buddha became divided. At the Council of Vesali, held about 350 B.C., there was a split in the monastic order.[5] One group of monks withdrew, protesting that the rules of the order were too strict. The more conservative elders believed that Buddhahood could only be attained through strict compliance with the rules of the monastic order as laid down in the *Vinaya-Pitaka*, or Rules of Discipline. From this group developed the sect called Theravada, Doctrine of the Elders. Theravada Buddhists believe that each individual must pass through many lifetimes and accumulate sufficient merit through his own efforts and good deeds in order to attain Nibbana. The ideal is the *arahat*, one who achieves Enlightenment through intense meditation.

The beliefs of the divergent group led in time to Mahayana Buddhism. This sect claimed the name Mahayana, meaning Greater Vehicle, and labeled all other sects Hinayana, or Lesser Vehicle. Mahayana Buddhists believe that it is possible for a man to attain Nirvana through devotion to Bodhisattvas and emulation of them. These are Buddhas-to-be, who have achieved through many lifetimes the ten virtues necessary to becoming a Buddha. The Bodhisattvas have delayed passing into Nirvana in order to help other men achieve a similar state of perfection, so that all may attain an end to rebirth.

According to Buddhist tradition, shortly after the Buddha's death a First Council was held at Rajagaha in northern India in order to recite his discourses.[6] At the Second Council at Vesali, mentioned above, the accepted body of doctrine, or canon, was divided into two *pitakas,* or baskets: the *Suttanta-Pitaka,* or sermons of the Buddha, and the *Vinaya-Pitaka,* rules of the monastic order.[7] When the schism between the two groups developed, the divergent group withdrew to hold its own council. In the *Dipavamsa,* a fourth-century-A.D. Sinhalese chronicle, the events of this dissident council are recorded.

The *Dipavamsa* reports that the attending monks altered and rearranged the canon, including the Jatakas.[8] This mention of them indicates that the collection of tales existed prior to the Council of Vesali, although it is not known what form the tales had at that time. In their oral transmission, it is thought, they were told as verses called *gathas,* although the verse may have been supplemented by prose.[9] Further evidence of their existence at this early date is found in other texts in which are listed the nine *angas,* or classifications of the oral canon, of which the seventh is Jataka.[10] The word jataka is found in writing on the stone fence which surrounds the the second-century-B.C. stupa, or reliquary mound, at Bharhut, where scenes from the stories are carved; this is the earliest written use of the word to have survived.[11]

In the third century B.C. the Third Buddhist Council was convened at Pataliputra under the patronage of King Asoka. At this time the doctrine was divided into three baskets: the *Suttanta-Pitaka* and *Vinaya-Pitaka,* mentioned above, and the *Abhidhamma-Pitaka,* a collection of texts dealing with Buddhist metaphysics and philosophy, which is considered by scholars to be a later addition to the canon.[12]

Shortly after the Third Council, around 250 B.C., Buddhism was taken to Ceylon by Mahinda, the missionary son of King Asoka. There, in the first century B.C., the Buddha's teachings were first committed to writing in Sinhalese, but this version no longer exists.[13] In the fifth century A.D., the Indian Buddhist monk and scholar Buddhaghosa went to Ceylon to edit and translate the scriptures into Pali.[14] Pali, one of the Prakrits, or spoken languages of India, had become the canonical and liturgical language of Theravada Buddhism. The scriptures are called the Pali canon or *Tipitaka,* meaning Three Baskets, the same three recited at the Third Council.

The *Suttanta-Pitaka,* the sermons of the Buddha, is divided into five sections called *nikayas,* or collections, the fifth of which is the *Khuddaka Nikaya,* comprising fifteen Buddhist texts, of which the Jataka is tenth. Within the Jataka, the 547 sets of verses are arranged in order of length into twenty-two groups, each called a *nipata.* The last group, consisting of the ten longest and most complex stories, is called the *Mahanipata,* or great *nipata.*

Not formally included in the Pali scriptures but of great importance to Buddhist philosophy are the commentaries on the canon, known in Pali as *atthakatha.* Many of those which accompany the scriptures of the fifth century were written by Buddhaghosa and other famed commentators but were apparently revisions of earlier commentaries.[15] The Jataka verses, or *gathas,* are embedded in prose, and the complete text is called the *Jataka-Atthakatha,* or the Jataka and its commentary. Although the Jataka commentary has been attributed to Buddhaghosa, scholars now believe that it was done by an unknown author at a slightly later date.[16] However, there is no doubt that whoever compiled the collection made use of older commentaries which no longer exist.[17] Because the verses are often unintelligible without the

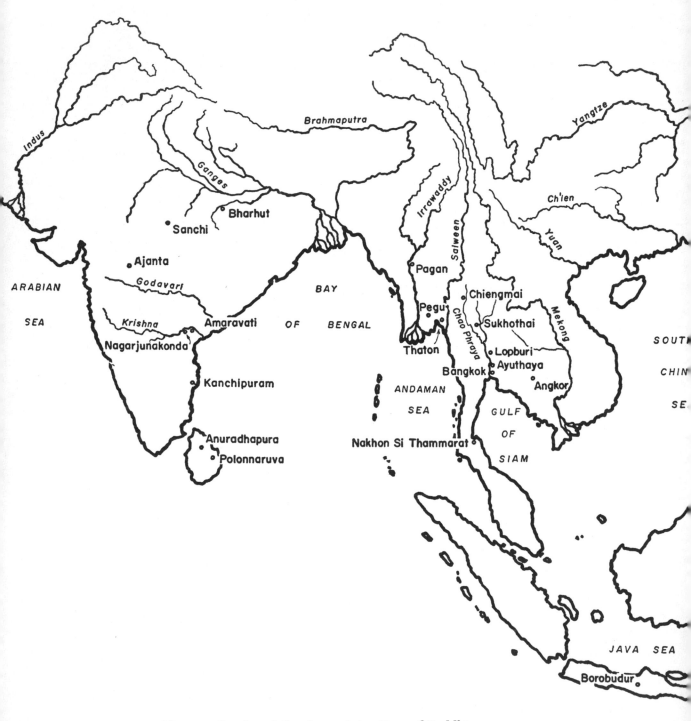

Map 1.   South and Southeast Asia: Sites of Buddhist monuments

accompanying narrative, the translation of the stories made by the Pali Text Society was of the complete *Jataka-Atthakatha*.

The stories in this text have a distinctive form which has come to be considered characteristic. First there is an introductory episode, an incident from the time of the Buddha which provides a reason for telling the tale. This is called the *paccupanna-vatthu*. Second, the narrative is related partly in verse and partly in prose; as the original verses are included here, this section is called by their name, the *atilavatthu*. The *veyyakarana*, a commentary, follows and is the Buddha's explanation of the meaning of the foregoing story. Finally there is the *samodhana*, or conclusion, when the Buddha returns to the present and identifies persons still living who are the later incarnations of the main characters.[18] In our retelling of the last ten Jatakas we have omitted the introduction, commentary, and conclusion, including only the narrative section.

SPREAD OF THE DOCTRINE   Buddhism had reached its greatest strength in India in the third century B.C. at the time of King Asoka. It remained strong through the reign of King Kanishka in the second century A.D., and then began slowly to decline. Brahmanism, the traditional religion of India, gradually regained its dominance. It acquired the name by which it is known today, Hinduism, and a new trinity of gods came to be worshiped: Brahma, Shiva, and Vishnu.

In the early centuries A.D., there were famous centers of Buddhist study such as Amaravati and nearby Nagarjunakonda in southern India, where monasteries filled with monks and scholars flourished under the protection of the Andhra kings. In the northwest, Taxila was a famed center of Buddhist studies. In the fifth and sixth centuries, thousands of monks meditated and studied in the monasteries of Kanchipuram in South India. From such renowned Buddhist cities missionaries voyaged to other parts of Asia, while other Asian Buddhists came to India, the home of the doctrine, to pursue their studies.

For many centuries India had been a great center of trade between East and West. Arab traders plied the seas to the West, transporting the exotic woods and spices that had been in great demand since the days of the Roman Empire. Indian traders traveled widely throughout the lands of Southeast Asia. Because strict Hindus considered themselves contaminated by contact with nonbelievers, many of the seafarers were Buddhists, who did not suffer from such restrictions.[19]

To facilitate the exchange of goods, trading settlements were established. Often the traders intermarried with the local people, perhaps with a chieftain's daughter, and established small Indianized kingdoms. Frequently, these acquired the trappings of Indian royalty, complete with Brahmin advisers, so that Hinduism existed alongside Buddhism in many small kingdoms in Southeast Asia.

After the fourth century, although Theravada Buddhism was no longer a significant force in India, it had become the foremost religion of Ceylon and had spread widely throughout Southeast Asia. Mahayana Buddhism was practiced longer in India, and this is the form that was taken overland to northern Asia, through Central Asia to China, Korea, and Japan.

The last stronghold of Buddhism in India was in the northeast, where it had originated, at the great university at Nalanda, which was a center of learning from the fourth to the twelfth century. When the Afghan armies of Muhammad Ghuri swept down from the north in 1197, they thought that the great walled city of learning was a fortress and that its orange-robed occupants were warriors, and therefore put the monks to the sword and left the city in flames. This gave the final blow to Buddhism in India, and it now exists only as a very minor sect among millions of devotees of Hinduism.

THE JATAKAS IN INDIAN ART   From the early centuries of Buddhism in India, the Jatakas were an inspiration to the painter and sculptor. This is attested by the remains of the stupas at Bharhut and Sanchi in central India and those at Amaravati and Nagarjunakonda in the south. Stupas, originally burial mounds, were built to house the holy relics of the Buddha and his disciples. They were sometimes surrounded by stone fences with great carved gates called *toranas,* covered with eloquent scenes of the life of the Buddha or from the Jataka tales. While the ten recounted here do not appear as a group, certain ones were clearly known and loved.

Carved on the ground railing of the stupa of Bharhut, dated to the second century B.C., are scenes from the Temiya Jataka, then called Mugapakkha; from an early version of Nimi called Makhadeva; from Mahajanaka; and from Vessantara.[20] Scenes from Mahosadha have also been identified.[21] At Sanchi, the Sama and Vessantara Jatakas appear respectively on the western and northern *toranas,* erected in the first century B.C.[22] Medallions and railings from the Amaravati stupa of the second century A.D. depict the Bhuridatta, Vidhura-Pandita, and Vessantara Jatakas;[23] a scene from Temiya has been identified, as well.[24] Among the second-century reliefs from Nagarjunakonda is one with scenes from Champeyya, an early version of Bhuridatta, and from Vessantara.[25]

In the west of India was the great monastery at Ajanta, where monks lived from the first century B.C. to the ninth century A.D., after which the cave temples were abandoned. They were rediscovered in the nineteenth century, and one can see there the evolution of the Buddhist cave temple, its interior glorified with sculpture and painting. Here, too, the Jataka tales are frequently represented in glowing murals; some of the most famous of the Ajanta paintings are scenes from the last ten Jataka tales. In cave ten, dated to the second century B.C., are depicted scenes from the Sama Jataka, painted as a frieze thought to have been done at about the same time.[26] Among the most famous are the fifth-century wall paintings which illustrate scenes from Mahosadha, also known as Maha-Ummagga, in cave sixteen, Vessantara in cave seventeen, and the Champeyya Jataka in cave one.[27] The Vidhura-Pandita Jataka appears in cave two, dated to the early sixth century.[28] Unlike the earlier paintings in cave ten, in which scenes succeed one another in a single row, each of these paintings covers a wall, with scenes distributed over the entire surface.

THE JATAKAS IN CEYLON   There are no remaining examples of early wall paintings or cloth paintings from Ceylon. However, in the *Mahavamsa,* a Sinhalese chronicle of the fifth century A.D., it is stated that in the second century B.C., King Dutthagamani ordered scenes from the Jatakas to be depicted around the inner relic chamber of the Ruanveli stupa at the capital city of Anuradhapura.[29] The author of the *Mahavamsa* also mentions that drawings of them were made on linen cloth with red arsenic.[30] However, there is no proof of the validity of these statements. Fa-hsien, a Chinese pilgrim of that time, wrote of having seen in Ceylon five hundred representations on silk and other cloths of the Buddha in his previous births.[31]

Although Buddhism was taken to Ceylon in the third century B.C. and the paintings were seen there as early as the second century B.C., today the oldest remaining wall paintings of the last ten Jatakas are those in the Tivanka Pilimage, or Northern Temple, at Polonnaruva, the capital of Ceylon from the eighth to fourteenth century.[32] The Tivanka Pilimage paintings, dated to the twelfth century, are thought to represent a continuation of ninth- to eleventh-century art at Sinhalese Buddhist monasteries at Mihintale and Mahiyangana, in which Jataka stories were among the most popular subjects of painting.[33]

Although in very poor condition today, the Tivanka Pilimage was once beautifully decorated with a scene of the Buddha descending from Tavatimsa heaven surrounded by worshiping devas and with scenes from the Jataka tales. In 1909, when the temple was studied and the murals were sketched, a number of Jatakas were depicted, including Temiya, Sama, Mahosadha, Vidhura-Pandita, and Vessantara.[34] The scenes were arranged in rows, with one story above another in no particular order.

From the fourteenth to the eighteenth century, when Kandy was the capital of a Ceylonese kingdom, many Buddhist temples were built and their walls decorated with Jataka tales in long narrow panels of continuous narration sometimes divided into rectangles. The Sinhalese painted scenes from many Jataka tales, including the last ten. In a temple built in the eighteenth century at Medawala, near Kandy, there are scenes from nine of the last ten Jatakas; only Mahosadha is missing.[35]

THE JATAKAS IN SOUTHEAST ASIA In Southeast Asia an early center of Buddhism was the kingdom of Srivijaya, which was centered in Sumatra but which at times ruled over parts of Java and the Malay peninsula. In the eighth and ninth centuries, the reigning dynasty in central Java was the Sailendra, a royal family possibly of Indian origin. The kings were Mahayana Buddhists who built the Borobudur, a tremendous stupa located in central Java. It is a magnificent structure erected in a series of tiers representing the Buddhist cosmology: lowest the world of desire, next the realms of form without desire, and at the top, symbolically represented, the world of formlessness. Each tier, with its accompanying balustrade, is embellished with beautifully carved panels. On one level of the wall around the structure, the story of the life of the Buddha is portrayed in stone relief. On this same tier and the one above are many carved scenes of Jatakas, including the Vessantara story.

From Khmer monuments in Cambodia and Thailand, we know that some of the Khmer kings also practiced Mahayana Buddhism. Notable among them was the last king of Angkor, Jayavarman VII, who considered himself a Bodhisattva and who built the Bayon, as well as many other temples, in honor of Buddhism. There is evidence that the Khmers were familiar with the Jatakas, for scenes from several, including Vessantara, are recognizable on pediments from the eleventh-century temples of Ta Nei and Prah Khan at Angkor.[36] Temiya, Sama, and Vessantara are portrayed on pediments of the twelfth-century Bayon, while other carvings from this temple have been tentatively identified as from Narada and Vidhura-Pandita, as well as Jatakas prior to the last ten.[37]

In Burma, before the Burmans descended from the mountains in the ninth century, the area was occupied by the Pyus, a Tibeto-Burman people who practiced Buddhism but who have since disappeared, and the Mons, linguistically related to the Khmers. In the eighth century the Mons, having eclipsed the Pyus, built a small but strong capital at Thaton in Lower Burma. By the eleventh century they had become Theravada Buddhists and maintained contacts with Ceylon. It is in Thaton that pictorial representations of the last ten Jatakas as a group first appear, dated to the eleventh century.[38] Collectively, they may be called by the name they hold in the Pali scriptures, *Mahanipata*.

The *Mahanipata* appears at three places in Thaton. The earliest description is from the Mon king Makuta's inscription at the Schwezayan stupa.[39] On the Thagya Paya stupa are fragments of terracotta tablets illustrating the last ten Jatakas, also depicted in stone carvings on the boundary pillars of an ordination hall called Kalyani Sima.[40] The tradition of decorating stupas with the Jatakas, and the last ten in particular, appears to have been a Mon tradition before Pagan became the capital of Burma.

In 1056 a monk named Shin Arahan, a Theravada Buddhist from Thaton, went to Pagan and converted King Anawrahta. He urged the king to ask Makuta, king of Thaton, for a copy of the *Tipitaka,* or Buddhist scriptures. When his request was denied, Anawrahta attacked Thaton, captured the Mon king, and brought back the scriptures by force. Hosts of monks and architects, painters, and other artisans were also taken to Pagan to depict in art King Anawrahta's newly adopted religion.[41]

Anawrahta built a number of religious structures. The Shwehsandaw stupa, dated 1060, is decorated with unglazed terracotta plaques illustrating the Jatakas, of which only fragments remain.[42] Of greater interest are the East and West Petleik stupas, dated to 1070. Each of these was decorated with a complete set of the Jatakas in unglazed terracotta plaques, each plaque inscribed with the name and number of the Jataka it illustrates. However, as the set numbers 550 and the numbering is different from the 547 stories of the *Jataka-Atthakatha* in the Pali scriptures, it may be assumed that the scriptures captured by Anawrahta in Thaton were not the Sinhalese Pali canon but perhaps another version of the scriptures.*

The next king, Kyanzittha, appears to have ordered a complete study and revision of the Buddhist scriptures based on the Sinhalese Pali canon, the *Tipitaka*.[43] Previously there had been strong elements of Mahayana Buddhism in Burma, but Kyanzittha supported Theravada Buddhism, which has prevailed in Burma ever since.

The plaques of the Jatakas on the Shwezigon, built early in Kyanzittha's reign, are arranged

* In *Old Burma–Early Pagan* (p. 40), Luce notes that the earlier, possibly South Indian recension in-includes three Jatakas following No. 496 (nos. 497, Velama; 498, Mahagovinda; and 499, Sumedhapandita), thus changing the numbering of the last fifty Jatakas and bringing the total to 550 (instead of the 547 in the *Jataka-Atthakatha* of the Pali canon). Further substantiation of the theory that the Burmese made use of another text of the Jatakas is offered in a study made by Ginette Martini entitled "Les Titres des Jataka dans les manuscrits pali de la Bibliothèque Nationale de Paris," *Bulletin de l'Ecole française d'Extrême-Orient*, vol. 51 (1963), pp. 79–90. This study of two undated manuscripts of Jataka tales in Pali from the collection of the Bibliothèque Nationale of Paris, one in Burman script, the other in Sinhalese, reveals significant differences in the order and titles of Jatakas, in particular of the last *nipata*. The dissimilarities in the two recensions indicate that the Burmese, and later the Siamese, had access to a text other than the Sinhalese Pali canon. Miss Martini points out that these differences are present in Cambodian and Laotian manuscripts of the Jatakas as well and suggests that the Buddhists of Indochina must have used a text or texts other than the Sinhalese Pali version.

in mixed order, suggesting the use of several texts of the scriptures simultaneously.[44] However, the order of the *Mahanipata* is the same as that on the Petleiks: Temiya, Mahajanaka, Sama, Nimi, Mahosadha, Canda-Kumara, Bhuridatta, Narada, Vidhura-Pandita, and Vessantara.

On the Ananda temple, Kyanzittha's masterpiece built in 1105, the Jatakas up to the last ten follow the numbering of the Sinhalese Pali canon.[45] However, the green-glazed terracotta plaques of the *Mahanipata,* appropriately located on the top level of the Ananda, are in the same order as those on the Petleiks. This sequence is also followed in similar plaques found on the uppermost terrace of the Mingalazedi stupa, built in 1250.[46] It would thus appear that for the last ten Jatakas, the builders adhered to the order traditionally used in the older temples of Pagan rather than the sequence of the stories in the Sinhalese Pali canon, which is slightly different: Temiya, Mahajanaka, Sama, Nimi, Canda-Kumara, Bhuridatta, Narada, Vidhura-Pandita, Mahosadha, and Vessantara.

The Jatakas also appear in wall paintings in the temples of Pagan. The interior walls of two temples built during Kyanzittha's reign, the Nagayon and the Abeyadana, are decorated with incomplete series of Jatakas previous to the last ten.[47] The Myinkaba Kubyauk-gyi temple, dated 1113, is thought to have been built under the supervision of Kyanzittha's scholarly son, Rajakumar. The Jatakas here are painted in squares in the Sinhalese manner. While fragmentary, they appear to follow the order of the Sinhalese Pali canon,[48] with the same exception in the last ten stories.

The most complete series of wall paintings of the *Mahanipata,* accompanied by inscriptions in old Mon, is in a small temple called the Lokahteikpan, built in the early twelfth century.[49] Its west wall is devoted to fourteen rows of panels of Jataka tales, of which the last ten rows depict the *Mahanipata.* The order in which the stories are painted, as opposed to that seen in the other temples mentioned above, is identical to the order used in the Pali scriptures. Most space is devoted to the last two Jatakas, Mahosadha and Vessantara, which are placed on the west and east side walls of the vestibule respectively. Presumably these two are given prominence because in the Pali canon they are the last two and also the most complicated of the stories.

Another type of religious painting that was common throughout the centuries was cloth banners, which could be hung from the walls of the temples. Being of perishable material, few are left that are more than two or three hundred years old. They may be seen in Ceylon today, with scenes painted in rows like temple murals. As the banners were easily transported, they were probably taken to Burma and other parts of Southeast Asia where Theravada Buddhism was practiced and where communication with the monasteries of Ceylon was frequent. Many monks from other parts of Southeast Asia also went there to study, as Ceylon was considered by Theravada Buddhists to have the oldest and the purest form of Buddhism.

THE JATAKAS IN THAILAND   Thought to have come originally from southeast China, the Thai peoples began moving southward at a very early date, gradually migrating into South China and present-day North Vietnam, perhaps even before the third century B.C., and from there moving farther south and west into Laos. Between the tenth and twelfth centuries they were migrating into Burma, where they were called Shans, and into northern Thailand.[50]

Before the arrival of the Thais, or Syam as they were called then, central and northern Siam were occupied by the Mon people, who by the sixth century had established a kingdom called Dvaravati. These Mons seem to have been Buddhists before their kinsmen in Burma. It is likely that they shared their fellow Mons' fondness for the Jataka tales, but so little remains of Dvaravati monuments in Thailand that evidence of this is scarce. A number of stucco reliefs removed from the Chula Pathon stupa near Nakhon Pathom, one of their principal cities, seem to represent Jatakas, but individual identifications have not been made.

The Thais, probably animists at that time, migrated gradually and peacefully into Thailand. By the twelfth century, there were large numbers of them living in northern Siam and around Sukhothai. In both Burma and Siam they must have been exposed to Mon culture and Theravada Buddhism, including the Jataka tales.

When Pagan was invaded by the Mongols in 1287, the power of the Burmese kingdom was temporarily destroyed. In nearby northern Siam, a Thai chief named Mengrai drove the Mon rulers from their small kingdom at Haripunjaya and established a new capital at Chiengmai. His kingdom was called Lan-Na.

At this time, most of the eastern part of present-day Thailand was ruled by the Khmer empire. In the middle of the thirteenth century, two Thai chieftains had rebelled against the Khmer rulers of Sukhothai in north-central Siam and established an independent kingdom. One of them became the first king of Sukhothai and was called Sri Indraditya.[51] The third king of Sukhothai, known as Ram Khamhaeng the Great, gained control over most of central and southern Siam. He was a strong king who established his rule over much of the former Dvaravati kingdom of the Mons as well as the Malay peninsula, Lower Burma, and parts of Laos.[52] He was also a Theravada Buddhist who maintained contact with the important center of Theravada Buddhism, Nakhon Si Thammarat in peninsular Siam. An inscription reads that King Ram Khamhaeng invited a worthy monk, learned in all the Three Baskets of the Buddhist scriptures, to come to Sukhothai from Nakhon Si Thammarat.[53] Close relations were also established with the Buddhist kingdoms in Burma. Ramannadesa, the Mon kingdom in Lower Burma, with principal cities at Thaton and Pegu, was a vassal of Sukhothai in Ram Khamhaeng's time.[54] Although it broke away after his death, religious interchange between the two states continued.

Ram Khamhaeng died about 1300 and was succeeded by his son Loe Thai, who reigned until 1346 and managed to lose most of the kingdom of Sukhothai.[55] During his reign, Theravada Buddhism as practiced in Ceylon was established in Siam. It appears that a number of monks went from Ramannadesa in Lower Burma to study at one of the most esteemed monasteries in Ceylon, the Udumbaragiri. On their return, they established a branch of this monastery at Pan near Martaban in Lower Burma. Some Thai monks went there from Sukhothai to study; when they returned to the Thai capital they founded a monastery where Sinhalese rites were performed. King Loe Thai welcomed them with great ceremony.[56]

It is in Sukhothai that the earliest evidence is found of the Jatakas in Thailand. At Wat Si Chum, the only building standing is a *mondop*, a square building housing an enormous image of the Buddha. Inside the thick walls of the mondop is a narrow passage which leads upward to the roof at a sharp angle. Fitted into the roof of the tunnel are one hundred slate slabs with Jataka scenes engraved on them. The scenes are from the first hundred Jatakas in the Pali canon and include early versions of two of the last ten, Mahajanaka and Nimi.[57] Some scholars think that these slabs were meant originally to be installed at Wat Mahathat, the principal monastery of the kingdom, probably founded by King Sri Indraditya in the thirteenth century.[58] It was rebuilt by King Loe Thai in the mid-fourteenth century to house some precious relics of the Buddha which had been brought by a Thai monk from Ceylon.[59] The slabs, in all likelihood made in Sukhothai but perhaps with the help of craftsmen from Ceylon, were engraved with delicate, simple lines; the figures are Sinhalese in appearance. It is now thought that the mondop at Wat Si Chum was subsequently built to receive the slabs in order to insure their safety in troubled times.[60] The engraved slabs fit the passageway so well that it seems to have been designed for them.

Loe Thai's son, Lu Thai, ruled Sukhothai from 1347 to 1374(?).[61] He was an able king in the face of a difficult situation. His father had lost most of the vassal states, and King Lu Thai struggled to regain them. He was serious scholar of Buddhism and wrote an important treatise on Buddhist cosmology called the *Traibhumi* (Three Worlds). In 1361 a learned monk from the monastery at Pan was installed as chief patriarch of Sukhothai, and King Lu Thai, announcing his resolution to be a Buddha, joined the monastic order for a period of several months.[62]

From 1380 dates an inscription found in Sukhothai which reads, "They listened to the Dhamma of the *Dasajati,* which was extremely sweet to hear."[63] Clearly the people of Sukhothai were familiar with the last ten Jatakas, which must have been told in the form of sermons as they are to this day.

According to the chronicles, Prince Uthong founded the city of Ayuthaya in 1350 and was crowned King Ramadhipati. He seems to have come from the Suphanburi region and fell heir to dominion over much of central Thailand. He and King Lu Thai agreed to respect each other's boundaries.[64] But after Lu Thai's death, Sukhothai became a vassal of the Ayuthaya kingdom and in 1438 was incorporated into it.[65]

Ayuthaya became a great city, filled with majestic temples and palaces, a center of commerce between east and west. However, in 1767 the Burmese armies poured across the plain, defeated the king of Ayuthaya, and raided the city, which caught fire and burned. Today little is left of its glory but the shells of its monasteries and stupas, lying neglected in the tall grass.

In what remains of Ayuthaya-period art and literature, evidence of the Jataka tales is scanty, though the Vessantara Jataka is mentioned in the annals. Here it is also recorded that in 1458 five hundred statues of Bodhisattas, representing the five hundred births of the Buddha, were cast on the occasion of a religious celebration.[66] Some of these figures can be seen today in the National Museum of Bangkok. From the lists of Buddhist texts used by King Lu Thai compiling the *Traibhumi,* it is clear that in the former capital of Sukhothai there had been a number of Buddhist manuscripts.[67] Since the Thai alphabet had been adapted from that of the Khmer during the reign of King Ram Khamhaeng, it is quite likely that parts of the Buddhist scriptures, perhaps including the Jatakas, were translated into Thai before and during the Ayuthaya period. However, there is no written version of the Jatakas in Thai dating from the Ayuthaya period.

One of the earliest pictorial representations of the last ten Jatakas in Thailand appears in a manuscript from the collection in the National Library, Bangkok. It is called the *Traibhumi* because its principal subject is the Three Worlds of Buddhist cosmology. It has been dated to the Ayuthaya period: probably the sixteenth or seventeenth century,[68] but perhaps as late as

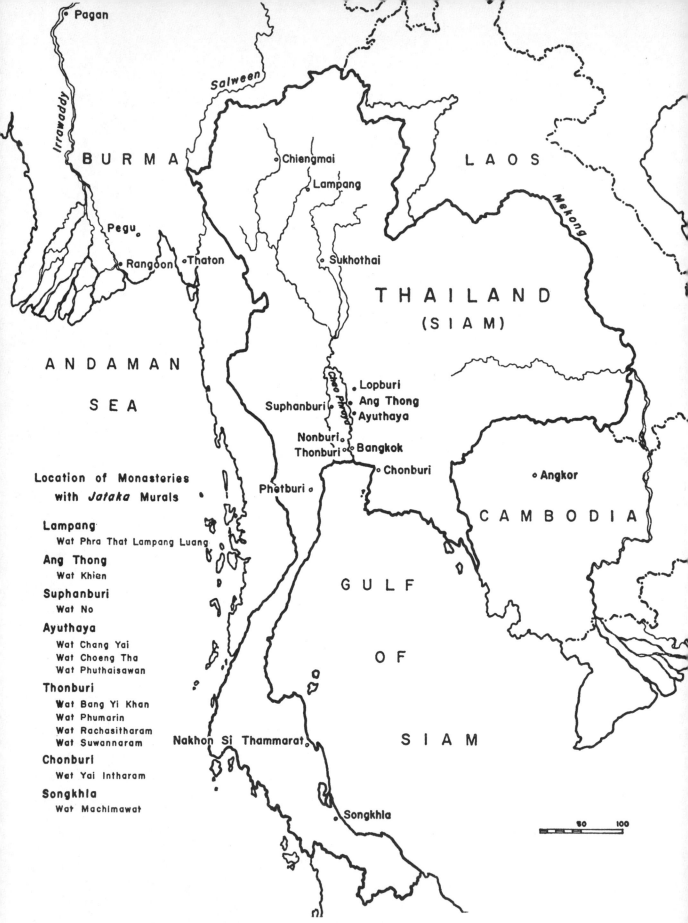

Map 2.   Thailand: Important historical cities and sites of monasteries with mural paintings

the eighteenth. In it, the order of the Jatakas is the same as that used on the Ananda and other temples in Pagan except that the story of Bhuridatta precedes that of Canda-Kumara.*

Few examples of wall painting are left from the Ayuthaya period. The walls of the lower crypt at Wat Rachaburana in Ayuthaya, dating from 1424, are covered with rows of paintings, including several scenes which are thought to represent Jataka stories previous to the last ten.[69] In the Patriarch's residence at Wat Phuthaisawan, however, are many scenes from the Buddhist scriptures, including the *Mahanipata*. Although only fragments remain, it is apparent that two of the four walls were devoted to illustrations of the last ten Jataka tales. The original buildings of Wat Phuthaisawan, one of the oldest monasteries in Ayuthaya, were erected in 1353 by the founder of Ayuthaya, King Ramadhipati. The Patriarch's residence was probably built later, at the end of the seventeenth century, and its paintings are dated to 1700.[70] It is the earliest example remaining of the use of the last ten Jatakas in mural art in Thailand. Many of the scenes used in later murals can be discerned here and are also to be found in the *Traibhumi* manuscript.

The stories of the *Mahanipata* were also used as the subject of temple decoration in stucco. At Wat Lai near Lopburi, a city north of Ayuthaya which has been an important center since the days of the Mons, there is a bas-relief of stucco over brick, attached to the end of the main hall of the monastery, depicting scenes from the last ten Jataka tales (see Fig. 5, page 130). The first five (Temiya, Mahajanaka, Sama, Nimi, and Mahosadha) are on the right side starting from the lower right corner; the second five (Bhuridatta, Canda-Kumara, Narada, Vidhura-Pandita, and Vessantara) on the left side beginning in the lower left corner. This sequence is the same as in the *Traibhumi* manuscript and at Wat Phuthaisawan; it is the order subsequently followed in Thai temple paintings.

In the center of the relief is a figure of the Buddha standing on a lotus. His right hand is raised against his chest with palm outward in a gesture of reassurance or protection. He is surrounded by hosts of devas in rows, while below him are a king and a queen on elephants, accompanied by attendants. The Buddha stands out because he is larger and in higher relief than the other figures. As one faces the building, the scene from Mahosadha is directly on the right of the Buddha and that from Vessantara on the left. Above each of them is a preaching scene, one from Nimi and one from Vidhura-Pandita. The effect is a pleasing mixture of symmetry and variety. The date of the stucco work is uncertain, but it appears to belong to the eighteenth century, or late Ayuthaya period.**

Thus, it seems that during the Ayuthaya period the custom of using the Jataka tales, especially the last ten, for decorating monastic buildings became popular in Siam. However, the

---

* A few other manuscripts from this period are known to exist but were not available for study.

** Personal communication from Hiram W. Woodward, Jr.: "Prince Damrong wrote that Wat Lai was restored during the reign of King Boromkot (1732–1758) (quoted in Huan Phinphan, *Lopburi thi no ru,* Lopburi, 1968, p. 123), but I have not found the source for the Prince's information. The manner in which the false mullions of the west face are cut out by angles recalls a similar feature at King Prasat Thong's Wat Chai Wathanaram (1630) and Nakhon Luang (1631), as well as at some other structures, but only a detailed study of late Ayuthaya wood-carving, which the decor at Wat Lai resembles, will allow us to date the Wat Lai stucco precisely. Unfortunately the date of the related stucco decor at Wat Nang Phya at Si Sachanalai is also unknown."

question remains: In the transmission of the Jataka tales to the Siamese which was more important, Burmese influence or direct contact with Ceylon?

In addition to the many religious contacts between Siam and Ceylon, there was considerable interchange between the Mon kingdoms of lower Burma and the Thai kingdoms of Lan-Na and Sukhothai, no great distance from each other. The great popularity of the Jatakas, especially the last ten, in temple decorations at Pagan, and the fact that the order of the last ten stories in the pictorial art of Siam is more similar to that of the temples at Pagan than to that of the Sinhalese Pali canon, strongly suggest that their popularity among the Thais was due to the religious interaction between the kingdoms of Siam and Burma during the Sukhothai and early Ayuthaya periods.

SIAMESE TEMPLE PAINTING

IN 1767, when Ayuthaya, capital of Siam for four hundred years, was conquered by the Burmese, the seat of the kingdom was moved south to Thonburi, and then in 1782 to Bangkok. The cities lie on either side of the Chao Phya River, called Maenam (mother of waters) by the Thai people.

Amid the noise and bustle of both cities are hundreds of oases of calm: the Buddhist temples, or *wats*. The royal monasteries are crowded with sightseers all day, while other monasteries serve as centers of community life. On Buddhist holy days, many people from the environs come to worship the Lord Buddha and to pay their respects to the monks.

Thonburi retains more than Bangkok the traditional atmosphere of Siam, with its busy canals, wooden houses on stilts, orchards, and gardens. Some of the older monasteries are here, often run-down and shabby but with traces of paintings on their walls. Others which have been renovated or built in recent times may be recognized by their brightly colored tile roofs and glass decorations that sparkle in the sunlight.

Beyond the twin cities extends the central plain of Thailand, emerald green with young rice during the summer rainy season, its flatness broken by tall, graceful palm trees. About fifty miles to the north of Bangkok lie the remains of the ancient capital of Ayuthaya. In north-central Thailand are the ruins of Sukhothai, the first capital of Siam.

In every village there are one or more wats, sometimes several quite close together. Surrounded by trees and an expanse of grass, the rectangular whitewashed buildings with steep roofs are usually simpler than the larger city temples. As they are often inconspicuous, hidden in a grove of trees at the far edge of a rice field, one is guided to them only by a glimpse of a curved roof finial or a flash of glazed tile. The village monasteries are usually small and may be built of wood or stucco-covered* brick with wooden architectural motifs.

---

* In Thailand, stucco is made from a mixture of "lime, sugarcane syrup, sand, and animal hide. The hide and syrup were boiled together and then mixed with water in which bark had soaked. The final mixture was used as mortar, for decorative stucco ornament and stucco images, and for coating wall surfaces." Mali Khokasanthiya, *Guide to Old Sukhothai,* trans. by Hiram W. Woodward, Jr. (Bangkok, 1971).

Although a few monasteries date back to the early centuries of the Thai kingdom, most of the religious buildings still in use were built in the last two or three hundred years. However, newer wats perpetuate many of the stylistic features of those built during the Ayuthaya period (ca. 1350–1767).

A THAI MONASTERY A lovely monastery compound may be found at Wat Suwannaram in Thonburi. Built in the early nineteenth century, Wat Suwannaram retains the characteristics of a traditional wat, although the exterior of the principal hall has been renovated.

As the religious area is surrounded by a wall, one must enter the compound through a gateway. Immediately one is struck with the imposing beauty of two large white rectangular buildings set on separate platforms about fifty feet apart in a square, paved courtyard. The two buildings are made of brick covered with white stucco. The building on the left has a green and orange tile roof of three layers which straddle each other (see Fig. 1, page 123). The apex of each layer rises slightly to a point and is crowned by wooden finials, shaped like abstract birds' heads with a hornlike element. They are called *cho fa* (sky tassel) for their apparent urge to reach the sky. Finials on the outer corners of the lower roof sections resemble multiheaded nagas, mythical serpents whose bodies form the undulating wooden bargeboards lining the edges of the triangular gableboard under the peak of the front porch roof. This serpent shape reappears on the many brackets below the eaves of the roof.

The importance of the building on the left is indicated by eight urn-shaped stones, called *sima* stones, enclosed in pointed encasements which surround the hall. A ninth stone is buried beneath the building itself. Their purpose is to mark off the boundaries of the consecrated property of the *sangha,* or Buddhist monastic order, and to identify the hall built upon that land as the *ubosot,* or *bot.* The bot, or ordination hall, houses the principal Buddha image of the monastery, in the presence of which ordination ceremonies take place.

The gableboard of the bot spans the area beneath the porch roof and bears delicate gilded wooden decorations, notably stemlike curling foliage designs out of which emerge the upper halves of devas with tall thin crowns. In the center of the gableboard is Vishnu riding the garuda, carved in high relief and backed by sparkling glass mosaics.

The building beside the bot is the *wihan.* Traditionally, this is where the laity gathers to hear the monks read the scriptures and explain the Doctrine. Informal talks with the monks may be held here, as well. However, the wihan at Wat Suwannaram is in need of renovation and is used as a library. The bot serves as a wihan in its stead.

Outside the bot and wihan but within the courtyard of the walled area are five white stucco stupas, or, as they are called in Thailand, *chedis.* In India, stupas were originally reliquary mounds containing relics of the Buddha or his disciples or were erected to commemorate sacred sites. In Thailand they rarely contain relics; they serve rather as symbols of the Buddha and often contain Buddha images, Buddhist texts, or treasures. Traditionally, chedis were the most important structures in a monastery; bots and wihans were originally built to accommodate the people who came to pay reverence to the chedis. Those at Wat Suwannaram, like many others today, are of a different type. They are mortuary stupas, donated by relatives of important personages and built over their ashes. Some monasteries have a *ho trai,* or special library to house the *Tipitaka,* within the walled courtyard, but none is evident here.

Fig. 1.   Exterior of the *bot* at Wat Suwannaram, Thonburi

Fig. 2.   Interior of the *bot* at Wat Suwannaram

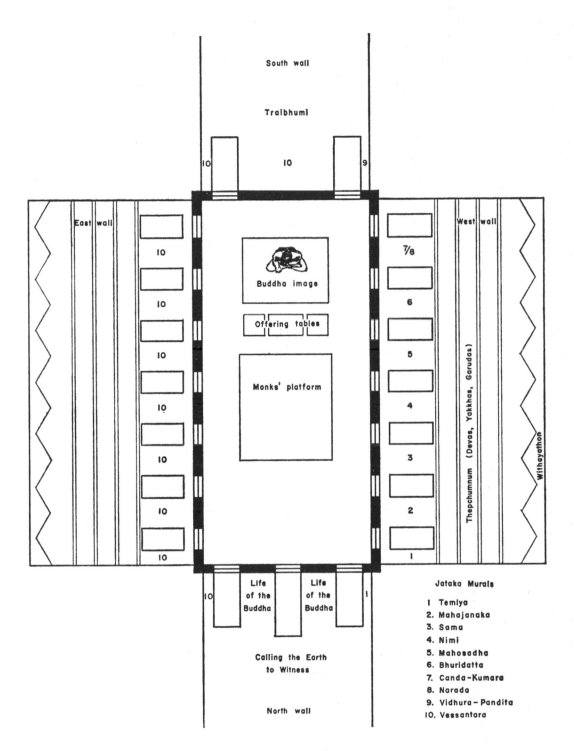

Fig. 3.   Interior of the *bot* at Wat Suwannaram

Beyond the white wall that designates the sacred area of Wat Suwannaram are other components of a Siamese monastery. Along the banks of the wide canal which the wat overlooks are *salas,* open-air roofed buildings, traditionally used as gathering places for the laity. A high platform with a many-layered Burmese-style roof is the crematorium, where part of the cremation ceremony takes place. A side gateway in the wall of the religious area leads to the *kuti,* or monks' living quarters, made up of rows of wooden houses on stilts surrounding a covered wooden platform. Next to the kuti is a tall bell tower set on large square tiers, whose bell is rung to call the monks to the daily ceremonies.

The entrance to the bot is from a small porch, through massive doors covered with elaborate designs in black lacquer and gold leaf. One's attention is first caught by an impressive Buddha image on a tiered pedestal at the rear of the hall (see Fig. 2, page 124). Two statues of standing disciples face the image.

The center of the bot is occupied by a low platform on which the monks kneel as they pay respects to the Buddha each day. In front of it is a square, carved wooden chair with cushions where the monk who reads the sermons sits cross-legged, holding the text of his discourse before him.

On the wall behind the Buddha image is a large scene of the *Traibhumi,* or Three Worlds of Buddhist cosmology. The lower portion of the wall above the doors is black, an appropriate background for the grotesque figures being tortured in gruesome scenes of the various hells. Above this level are pictured the woodlands and animals of the Himavat. Extending upward in painted columns from the forest are mountain peaks upon which rest the palaces of the gods in Tavatimsa heaven. The tallest peak, in the center, supports the palace of Sakka, within which the green-skinned king of the gods presides over a company of celestial maidens. On either side of the columns of mountains are the oceans, filled with marine animals of all kinds. To the far right and left respectively are the yellow moon and the red sun.

This scene of the *Traibhumi* serves as a background to a major scene from the life of the Buddha: the descent of the Buddha from Tavatimsa heaven. Having preached to his mother in Sakka's heaven, he is returning to earth. As he descends the ladder, the gods Brahma and Sakka hover in attendance. On this occasion a miracle occurred in which the heavens, the world of men, and the hells were visible to each other, so figures from these worlds are shown, the palms of their hands joined to form the Eastern gesture of reverence.

The side walls above the windows are lined with traditional *thepchumnum,* celestial beings kneeling in reverence. There are four rows of white-skinned devas, green-colored yakkhas, and pink-skinned garudas alternating with one another and separated by fans against a red and dark blue background. A jagged feathery line separates the top row from some strange figures above it: men dressed as hermits, called *withayathon.* Thought to have reached these heights through magic or intense meditation, they are seen rushing about the clouds, flying, dancing, gesturing, or running off with damsels under their arms.

The space on the front wall between the top of the front doors and the ceiling is covered with an action-filled scene of the Buddha subduing Mara, the king of evil, and his demons. The Buddha figure is seated cross-legged, touching his right hand to the ground. With this gesture, he is calling upon beautiful, sinuous Dharani, the Earth Mother depicted below, to acknowledge his right to Enlightenment. She does so by wringing out her hair, thus producing a flood which dispels the forces of evil. The tremendous amount of water represents the innumerable times the Buddha has dispensed charity in his former lives. These gifts were indicated by pouring water upon the hands of the receiver, and thus upon the earth. Dharani releases all the water she has been given in the previous lifetimes of the Buddha, symbolizing his boundless generosity. On the right side of the Buddha, Mara is seen on elephant-back attacking with his armies. On the left, his forces are in a state of disarray as they are swallowed up by the flood waters. Mara bows in reverence to the Buddha, to whom the elephants offer lotus flowers with their trunks.

Between the seven windows on each side are scenes from the last ten Jatakas (see Fig. 3, page 125). Nine are on one wall, while the Vessantara Jataka covers the other wall as well as the space between the back doors. The space between the three front doors is decorated with two panels of scenes from the life of the Buddha, one of the Great Departure, when the Buddha as Prince Siddhattha, having left his family and kingdom, rides off into the night. The other scene depicts him cutting off his long hair, thus severing his ties with the secular world before becoming an ascetic.

SIAMESE PAINTING: A REVIEW The oldest wall paintings remaining in Siam are found in dark and remote places not frequented by the laity. That they have been preserved may be attributed to their location. Dating from the late thirteenth century are some fragmentary paintings in the Silpa cave at Yala in southern Thailand and at Wat Chedi Chet Thaew at Si Sachanalai near Sukhothai.[1] Similar murals, from the fifteenth century, were found at Ayuthaya, in the now collapsed Phra Prang at Wat Mahathat and in the crypt of the eastern stupa at Wat Phra Si Sanphet.[2] They were not painted to be viewed but were intended as offerings, to make merit for the donor who commissioned them.

The subject matter was the same as that which has been found in much of the sculpture and painting at Ajanta in India, at Anuradhapura in Ceylon, and at Pagan in Burma: rows of seated Buddha figures either in meditative posture, their legs crossed, hands resting in their laps one upon the other with palms up, or calling the earth to witness, with the right hand touching the earth; or rows of standing disciples and devas. In Siamese paintings such figures often flanked the painted Buddha figure, kneeling toward the Buddha, their palms held together in adoration.

The facial features and crown details of these haloed beings and the subtle variety in tilting heads are reminiscent of frescoes seen in Ceylon in an eighth-century crypt at Mihintale and an eleventh-century crypt at Mahiyangana. Such Sinhalese features are also present in the engraved slabs of Jatakas at Wat Si Chum in Sukhothai. Indeed, a current of Sinhalese influence in Thai art was inevitable, considering the value placed upon Sinhalese Buddhism by Siamese kings of the Sukhothai period and the presence of Sinhalese monks and craftsmen in Sukhothai at that time.

Two crypts in the major *prang* (shrine) at Wat Rachaburana of Ayuthaya, dating from 1424, reflect some experimentation with content and style. While two walls of the upper crypt bear traces of traditional flying devas, reflecting Sinhalese influence in posture as well as faces, crowns, and haloes, two other walls have sketches of Chinese soldiers and an oversized Chinese guardian figure with a round "evil eye." The guardian appears to be frightening away children, although some scholars claim that he is meant to be a god of prosperity.[3] The large dimensions of these figures and the addition of the color pink to the usual red, black, and yellow used in previous paintings are unusual. From this crypt alone, then, it may be ascertained that early Siamese painting was subject to both Sinhalese and Chinese influences.

The lower crypt is a very small chamber only about six feet square, with a niche for a Buddha image on each side. Its high walls are covered with painted figures on a reddish ground. The paintings are mostly in rows and are occasionally divided into squares; both of these formats are common to Sinhalese and Burmese paintings. The top row is filled with Buddha figures. Below them are rows of disciples and scenes from the life of the Buddha and from Jataka tales,[4] too fragmentary to be identified with accuracy. All the figures are delicately outlined in black or red and filled in with white, gold, or brown.

The lower crypt is the only remaining example of narrative wall painting before the eighteenth century. Once filled with Buddha images and treasure, the crypt was sealed; it is therefore unlikely that the murals exerted an influence on the subsequent development of Thai art, although they probably indicate the quality of Thai painting at the time they were made.

By the mid-eighteenth century, there must have been hundreds of majestic temples in Ayuthaya. Most of them were destroyed in the Burmese invasions of 1767. Since then, the tropical climate with its high humidity and heavy rains, the leaky temple roofs, and soluble paints have all contributed to the continuous deterioration of the murals. As a result, it is nearly impossible to trace the evolution of Thai painting with certainty.

On the basis of the vestiges remaining, it appears that Buddha figures and disciples, in separate horizontal rows, were the primary subjects for wall paintings during most of the Ayuthaya period. Additional symbols of the Buddha were added to separate the figures in rows from each other: leaf- or flame-shaped fans, stupas, multi-tiered umbrellas, and bodhi trees. Worshiping figures were also painted in rows covering the entire wall. Called thepchumnum, they included garudas and yakkhas alternating with devas as they knelt in reverence facing the Buddha statue at the rear of the building. The first example of these rows of heavenly beings is found in Phetburi, a city in peninsular Siam, at Wat Yai Suwannaram,[5] dating to at least the first half of the seventeenth century.[6] The figures, nearly two feet in height, are separated by jagged-line dividers and floral patterns, two of the earliest artistic motifs in Thai painting. On both sides of the jagged lines are fringelike stripes.

Such murals, through the repetition of figures in rows, contributed to a solemn meditative atmosphere within the hall. The monks and laity modeled themselves after the painted worshipers as all knelt facing the Buddha image.

Apart from the murals at Wat Rachaburana, no one knows exactly when narrative themes began to occur in mural art, but during the first half of the eighteenth century, scenes from the life of the Buddha and from the last ten Jataka tales were painted.

The earliest example of the last ten Jataka tales in wall painting is in the residence of the Patriarch at Wat Phuthaisawan, which was constructed in the compound of the fourteenth-century monastery in about 1700. The paintings of the ten tales reveal a delicate simplicity of line, subdued colors (except in palace scenes, where the dominant color is red), and a talent for finely detailed landscape that is used to frame scenes. In some tales there are large architectural forms whose dominance, through a form of aerial perspective, reflects some Chinese influence. Some of the remaining scenes from the Mahajanaka and Vessantara Jatakas, such as

Fig. 4. Interior of the *bot* at Wat Yai Intharam, Chonburi. Shown here is a portion of the right-hand side wall with an overall view of the Sama, Nimi, and Mahosadha Jatakas. This wall shows three rows of *thepchumnum*. Of the three Jatakas depicted, the Nimi Jataka is the clearest. Massive round columns with designs painted in red and gold lacquer support the roof. In the foreground is the monks' platform. For a detail of the Sama Jataka, see Plate 9, page 45. An overall view of the Nimi Jataka is seen in Plate 11, page 46.

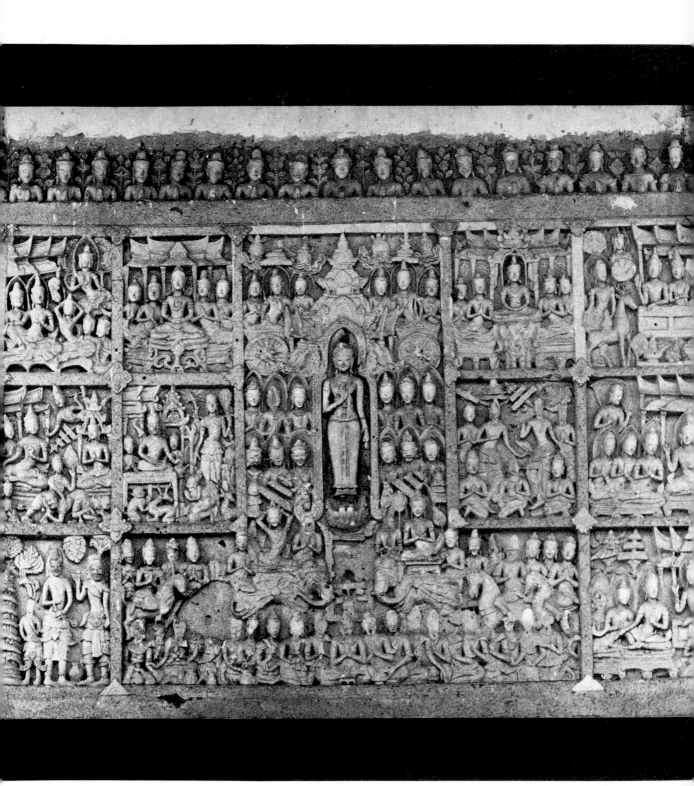

Fig. 5.   Scenes in stucco of the last ten Jataka tales, at Wat Lai, Lopburi

Mahajanaka being recognized by Brahmins as their king (see Plate 7, page 39), and two from Vessantara, are the same in theme and certain stylistic details as later mural paintings.

The next example of the Ten Lives in temple painting is at Wat Prasat in Nonburi, dating from 1750. Between the Jatakas in the windowless bot are tall worshiping devas, forerunners of the figures painted on the window shutters of later wats. Above this level is a large band of traditional seated Buddha figures with kneeling disciples and tiered umbrellas on either side. The paintings of the Jatakas demonstrate how, in the Ayuthaya period, artists divided scenes with uneven jagged lines and filled space with decorative many-petaled flowers, large palace scenes, and rows upon rows of people kneeling, squatting, or walking. Such groups of either worshipers or soldiers, depending upon the story, formed horizontal bands across the picture space. This was not unlike the convention used in narrative painting at Pagan, nor was it far from the Thais' own traditional rows of disciples and devas. In later murals of the Bangkok period, muralists incorporated such rows of figures in ways more relevant to the tales and more harmonious to the setting, such as royal processions (see Plate 32, page 102).

In addition to fragments of wall painting from the thirteenth to the eighteenth century, two important records of the evolution of Siamese painting remain, though few in number: manuscripts and cloth banners. Sometime after the fifteenth century, when paper had been introduced to Thailand, artists began to illustrate manuscripts. Although the oldest Siamese manuscripts were inscribed with a stylus on long narrow strips of dried palm leaves, those which were illustrated were done on long strips of *khoi* paper, a type of soft cardboard made from the pulp of the *khoi* plant.* Manuscripts depicting the Three Worlds of Buddhist cosmology were called *Traibhumi* after the fourteenth-century treatise by King Lu Thai. The one we have studied from the National Library is about 21¼ inches in width and 59 feet 3 inches in length. It is folded back and forth until it resembles a flat accordion of about 8¼ inches across.[7] Some writing may be found across the illustrations, mostly in the form of labels.

The paintings in this manuscript illustrate the various levels of the universe, with diagrams of the world of men leading to the imaginary Himavat forest and the heavens above. Narrative scenes include the last ten Jataka tales, with a set of thirteen scenes of the Vessantara story; the life of the Buddha; and Thai folktales, notably the *Manohra* tale. The Ayuthaya-period manuscript has been tentatively dated to the mid-sixteenth century,[8] but striking resemblances in themes, specific scenes, and style between it and paintings of the late Ayuthaya period and early Bangkok period may indicate that the manuscript dates to the late Ayuthaya period. Fearing that the art of manuscript illumination would be lost, in 1776 King Taksin ordered that a copy of the Ayuthaya *Traibhumi* be made. This version, called the Thonburi *Traibhumi*, may also be seen in the National Library in Bangkok but differs from the earlier one in style. A similar manuscript of the Thonburi period is owned by the Berlin Museum.[9]

From an inscription of Wat Jan Lom dated 1384, it appears that cloth banners were used in Thailand as early as the Sukhothai period.[10] A pious man called the Foster Father Sai Tam, who was close to King Lu Thai, converted his home into this monastery.[11] In order

---

* The khoi plant is *Streblus asper*. See Silpa Bhirasri, *The Origin and Evolution of Thai Murals* (Bangkok, 1959), p. 32.

to make merit for others and himself, the Foster Father chose a number of artists to "come and compose paintings of *devatas* and *asuras* and of an ordination together with a throng of monks, beautiful in every detail."[12] He "also had a Chinese cloth picture of the Buddha brought and installed" which "he raised up . . . to a height of 14 cubits. . . ."[13]

Cloth banners which date to the Ayuthaya period are few; the most numerous date to the nineteenth century.[14] The earliest cloth banners depict scenes from the life of the Buddha and hieratic scenes of the standing Buddha flanked by two disciples. Those of the Bangkok period include scenes from the last ten Jatakas, either individually or all together on one banner. The ceremony of reciting the Vessantara Jataka* throughout two or three holy days a year is accompanied by a set of banners illustrating the story which are unfurled for that occasion only. In general, the painting style of banners evolved alongside that of mural and manuscript painting, though each genre had its own idiosyncrasies.

THE THAI PAINTER   To be a painter of religious art was a worthy career, and the Thai painter demonstrated patience and devotion to his craft. A master artist, whether monk or layman, was highly respected. An apprentice proved his loyalty to his master and to the art of painting in the annual *wai khru* (paying respects to teachers ceremony). This meant honoring the memory of past generations of teachers, as well. When a master artist died, his brushes, sketchbooks, mortars, pestles, and other tools were highly venerated by his family; if he had been a monk, these implements were kept in a monastery until a successor was deemed worthy to use them. Often apprentices were drawn from the family of a master artist.

The initiation of the apprentice into the world of Thai art was a gradual process. At first he was allowed to carry out only the most menial chores, such as the long process of making paint. Before the eighteenth century, when paints began to be imported from China in powder form, natural colors were taken from riverbed clays. These colors were similar to those used in Burma and Ceylon: white, yellow, and red. The apprentice had to remove the gravel and foreign matter from the clay before it could be dried and pounded to fine powder. To apply it to the dry wall surface, the painter bound the pigment with a precise amount of either strained tree gum or animal glue. Too much glue caused the colors to crack; too little caused them to blur.[15] In addition to the earthen pigments, some greens could be made from pulverized plant stems, and blacks came from soot. Gold leaf pounded from Thai gold into thin sheets was also applied to paintings with a sticky tree sap to highlight the crowns, jewelry, and other accouterments of royalty.

The next thing the apprentice may have learned was how to make brushes. The process consisted of cutting bark from special trees and roots. The bark was soaked in water, then flattened, shredded, and cut away at the tip. Round brushes were made from the aerial roots of a mature tropical plant. After the core of the root was shredded and the pieces arranged into a thick

---

* In Thailand this ceremony, which occurs between October and December, is called the *Thet Maha-chat,* or Sermon of the Great Birth Story. It is believed that if one hears the entire recitation, which lasts several days from morning till late at night, one will accumulate a great amount of merit. See Phya Anuman Rajadhon, *Essays on Thai Folklore* (Bangkok, 1968), p. 168.

circular brush, it could be used for painting trees and shrubs. Very fine lines were made with brushes of hair from the inner ear of a cow.[16]

Once the pigments were prepared and the brushes ready, the master artist had to be sure the walls were ready to paint. Unlike the Western fresco technique, in which pigments were applied rapidly to a wet plaster surface, for the tempera method used in Thailand and Burma the wall surface had to be thoroughly dry for paint to adhere to it. In preparation, the wall was washed numerous times with a solution of desalinated limewater, to which fine sand and sugar had been added, and allowed to dry between washings. It was then splashed with a solution of water and pounded vegetable leaves in order to remove all traces of salt from the surface. This drying and splashing process continued for about fifteen days, until the wall tested negatively to being rubbed by a yellow turmeric root called *khamin*. If the root turned red, the surface was not yet ready for the next step; if the root remained yellow, it was. Next, several coatings of white chalk mixed with paste made from roasted tamarind seeds were smoothed on, one coat at a time, so that each coat could dry before the next was applied. The gummy pigments would then adhere to the wall, and the painter could begin.[17]

Unfortunately, the process was neither very durable nor waterproof, and as a result of climatic and social conditions, much of Thai mural painting has been lost. The photographs in this book are taken from those murals still in good enough condition to be worthy of reproduction. They are drawn from a number of wats scattered throughout Thailand, from Lampang in the north to Songkhla in the south. Most of the photographs are from wats painted in the first, second, or third reigns of the present dynasty, that is, between 1782 and 1851: wats Bang Yi Khan, Rachasitharam, and Suwannaram in Thonburi; Wat Yai Intharam in Chonburi; and Wat Machimawat in Songkhla. The murals from Wat Phra That Lampang Luang in Lampang may date to the eighteenth century, although the wat itself was founded many centuries previously. Unlike the other wats already mentioned, here the paintings are done on high narrow wooden walls of a wihan which, like those of other northern Thai wats, is open at the sides. The roof and walls of the building are supported by large wooden columns. The paintings in wats No in Suphanburi, Phumarinrachapaksi in Thonburi, Khien in Ang Thong, and Choeng Tha and Chang Yai in Ayuthaya were painted in the mid-nineteenth century, between 1850 and 1875, but are traditional in style.

NARRATIVE COMPOSITION Unlike Western painting, a Thai illustration of a story is rarely devoted to just one episode. A number of scenes, chosen for their action, humor, or moral lesson, tell the tale. Like the early Buddhist sculpture and painting of India, which remain its ultimate source, this is an art of continuous narrative, in which the same character is repeated in several scenes. Unlike the *Traibhumi,* in which the Jatakas are arranged into squares of four scenes or rectangles of two scenes per story, divided horizontally by ribbon-like bands filled with stylized waves, and unlike Sinhalese and Burmese paintings of the Jatakas, in which scenes are crowded into rows or squares, in Thai murals the scenes are distributed over an entire panel. Two or three Jatakas may even share the area of a single panel.

Scenes are not placed in chronological sequence; rather, they are arranged according to where they occur. For example, even though Sama being wounded and Sama being mourned are two incidents separated in time by several events, they are painted in the same locale, the forest. Moreover, an episode from the previous Jataka, Mahajanaka, which is on the same panel as the Sama Jataka, shares the same backdrop, without a jagged line or other strong divider indicating that this is from another story (see Plate 8, page 40).

The ways in which scenes are kept separate and background space is filled depend upon when the painting was executed, the amount of space to be covered, the imagination of the artist, and the degree of his interest in compositional unity. Scenes were often divided by a jagged, feathery line (see Plate 11, page 46). The jagged-line motif led to a later, more sophisticated means of organizing the wall space: irregular architectural forms such as palace rooftops, crenellated walls, and zigzag screens (see Plate 25, page 87). Landscape is equally important in this regard. Angular hills, pointed mountains, shrubbery, flowering trees, rubbery boulders, rocks, and cliffs—all these features were used both to separate scenes and fill background space. The artist took delight in rendering them in detail, down to the last leaf of the trees. Landscape elements sometimes appear to conform to a character's bodily lines, echoing his curves (see Plate 29, page 96).

The ways in which perspective is handled in Thai painting emphasize the separateness of scenes on a panel. Whereas in the *Traibhumi* figures and other elements of the painting are placed side by side or above one another, parallel to the picture plane, in murals a form of aerial perspective is used in addition to this convention. Probably introduced by Chinese craftsmen in the early eighteenth century, this technique is already evident in some of the murals at Wat Phuthaisawan, dating from ca. 1700.

If one looks at the overall painting of the Temiya Jataka at Wat Yai Intharam (see Plate 1, page 27), one can see that there is an inconsistency between the depth of the palace courtyard and the relatively flat forest scenes. In the judgment scene (see Plate 2, page 28) a sense of three-dimensional space is created in the foreground by the shape and position of the crenellated wall. Because the wall is low and the figures within it are visible, one has the impression of looking down into the courtyard from somewhere above the scene. At that point three-dimensional space ends and except for the throne, which juts out at a slight angle from the palace, the rest of the scene is painted in horizontal strips above and behind one another: the facadeless interior is made up of red and blue vertical bands, a jagged-edged screen with floral designs, and trees that seem to grow from the architecture itself.

From the judgment scene, one moves right and downward to two torture scenes separated by an artificial line and appearing to be framed in little pockets of space. The crenellated wall brings the viewer back to the uppermost scenes: Temiya lifting the chariot and the king visiting his son at the hermitage (see Plate 3, page 28). Altogether, the picture space is broken up into a number of segments, compelling the spectator to view the mural slowly, scene by scene.

Within scenes themselves, the figures are often arranged in harmonious groupings. When Temiya lifts the chariot to test his strength and the gravedigger and the horses twist themselves around, all three elements form an aesthetically pleasing triangular unit (see Plate 4, page 33). A vaguely outlined gray mountain serves to make the figures seem to be detached from the earth. The scene at Wat Bang Yi Khan of Sama's parents, a goddess, and kinnari maidens lamenting over Sama's body is a charming one (see Plate 10, page 45). The figures form a triangle in which most of the crowned heads bend in one direction, while the mourning gesture is gracefully echoed.

In 1851, when King Mongkut, also known as Rama IV, mounted the throne, the government of Siam turned from its former policy of isolation to improved relations with foreign nations. It was then that Western influence on Thai painting began to be felt, especially in murals in the urban areas. For example, a vanishing point appeared, and figures were made to diminish in size as they receded into the background. Before that time, a horizon line was sometimes created merely by the point at which stylized waves ended and blue sky began, not by any systematic recessional movement in the painting (see Plate 6, page 34). Also, before the 1850's overlapping of figures existed in both manuscript and mural art, but the figures never varied in size according to their location.

REPRESENTATION OF FIGURES   While composition and landscape have varied with the times, the depiction of human beings has remained fairly consistent. From the earliest examples, Thai pictorial art has been distinguished by an elegant linear style; the outline and details of each figure are defined by smooth, often curving lines. All creatures have a flat, two-dimensional appearance, as if they had been cut out of cardboard, with their joints strung together like those of shadow puppets, revealing no trace of bones, veins, or muscles. The artist conveys the spiritual nature of a character by adhering to a prescribed artistic vocabulary. What we see is a hierarchy based on the degree of spiritual advancement of each class of beings.

On the highest levels are the Bodhisatta, devas, ascetics, and royal personages. Accordingly, they wear pleasant, masklike expressions. It would be a sign of moral inferiority to reveal an emotion on one's face. Once an individual is born into a high level of society or lives a hermit's life, he is assumed to have overcome base feelings like anger and greed and to have achieved an inner calm.

This calm is often expressed by a profile view. The invariable set of features includes an arched eyebrow ending in an inverted comma, a graceful, elongated lotiform eye and eyelid, a long narrow nose with a high nostril, a curving moustache line above thick, slightly pursed lips, and two comma-like chin lines. Kings are usually seen in this profile view (see Plate 32, page 102).

The face of the Bodhisatta figure, as of queens and goddesses, is generally shown in a three-quarter view, and the features are softer, reflecting a more tranquil nature. Despite his great physical strength, the Bodhisatta is a gentle being of whom even the deer are not afraid. His expression, always youthful and peaceful, indicates his great moral purity, and his eyes are usually lowered, while a faint smile may touch his lips. When he is seen in front view, his features are symmetrically arranged. When Mahajanaka is about to be scooped up from the sea, both he and the goddess Manimekhala bear the same facial features in three-quarter view (see Plate 6, page 34).

Commoners, on the other hand, who are thought to be of a more bestial nature, do not control their facial expressions, which may be quite grotesque. Their supposed moral inferiority is an excuse for artists to let themselves go in scenes which may be quite licentious but where a raucous vitality is also present. Sturdy-looking, and wearing only loincloths, with bandanas around their heads, commoners are often engaged in manual labor, with limbs at awkward angles and heads twisted around (see Plate 4, page 33), or kneeling before their sovereign, the orbs of their bottoms facing us (see Plate 2, page 28). Contrasting with the rigid and formal portrayal of the more elevated personages in the tale, they provide a welcome comic relief.

Thai artists seem to have adhered to traditional concepts of beauty originally derived from Indian canons of idealized form.[18] Certain features, such as lotiform eyes, bowlike brows, lime-shaped chins, and arms resembling a young elephant's trunk, distinguish sculptured and painted figures of the Buddha, Bodhisattas, devas, and royalty.

Royal figures and devas are also set apart by halos, elaborate crowns, tiered umbrellas, and their gold-leafed palaces with overlapping roofs. Sakka, king of the gods, is green-skinned and carries a thunderbolt and mallet, reminiscent of his origin as the Vedic god of thunder, Indra. Queens and goddesses wear crowns which may reveal one or two sections of hair beneath; kings' crowns cover the entire head.

In general, royal costumes resemble the attire of the kings and queens of the Ayuthaya period. In the interest of design, not realism, folds of skirts hang in even accordion pleats, and tail ends of sashes balance each other symmetrically at either end of the waist or ankles (see Plate 9, page 45). Women appear to wear tight-fitting trousers, which are merely skirts tucked up between their legs. They are bare-breasted, with a sash over one shoulder.

Ascetics may be recognized by their spotted leopard-skin skirts and capes and blunt-edged headdresses (see Plate 29, page 96). Brahmins, when cast in a villainous role, like Jujaka in the Vessantara story or Alambayana in the Bhuridatta Jataka, appear old, scrawny, and ugly, often with bumps on their faces, and wearing loincloths and bandanas (see plates 18, page 65; 19, page 66; and 29, page 96). When they are reputable members of the court, as in the Mahajanaka Jataka, they are less unkempt and their facial features are less exaggerated (see Plate 7, page 39). But their faces are always lined with wrinkles, and their hair is tied low behind their heads.

Semidivine mythical animals of the Himavat have varied features drawn from the real world, artists' imaginations, and traditions of India and the Near East. Nagas, when in human form, are recognizable by their crowns edged with cobra hoods (see Plate 19, page 66); or they may appear as serpents with jagged teeth and a cock's comb (see Plate 18, page 65). Garudas, the great birds, may have human features from neck to waist, along with beaks, feathers, and claws distinguishing them as birds (see Plate 17, page 65). They may also be seen in human form, with only a suggestion of feathers lining their arms. The male kinnara and female kinnari are a combination of the lower half of a *hamsa* (mythical goose), with short thin legs, claws, scaly wings, and a *kranok,** or flame-shaped, tail, and the upper half of a human being (see Plate 10, page 45).

The giants, yakkhas, have demonic faces with bulging eyes and bulbous noses, fangs, and pointed ears (see Plate 24, page 87). Actual creatures like the elephant, horse, rabbit, and deer are drawn with skill and charm. The distinguishing marks of each are emphasized with a childlike simplicity. All animals, whether exotic or real, are portrayed with humor and verve in their stylized movements.

* The *kranok* is thought to symbolize the flame of Buddhism purifying mankind of the three defilements: greed, aversion, and delusion.

Foreigners were not considered a part of this hierarchy, and their facial features are very individualized. Whether they are Chinese mandarins in long robes and trailing whiskers or Caucasians wearing tricorn hats and tall boots, their national features are exaggerated and, with their swords or guns in hand, they appear alternately arrogant, weary, and ferocious (see plates 13 and 15, pages 58 and 60). They frequently appear in the Mahajanaka Jataka as the luckless sailors who are swallowed up by the sea and ferocious fish (see Plate 6, page 34). It is not surprising that they are found in abundance in Thai painting, for there have been Asian traders in Thailand for many centuries and Europeans since the fifteenth century.

Lowest in the hierarchy are those unfortunate ones who suffer in the various hells. In the Nimi Jataka, their features are distorted and nonhuman, ghostly figments of a tortured imagination. Sometimes headless, sometimes bodiless, they are seen being burned in caldrons of boiling water, pierced with hooks and spears, or disemboweled in grotesque ways (see Plate 11, page 46).

In mural paintings up until the introduction of narrative art, postures rarely varied except for the changing angle of the face from side to three-quarters to front. The Bodhisatta figure in paintings of the Jatakas is found in a few postures characteristic of the Buddha figure of non-narrative art and sculpture. When meditating, he sits cross-legged, hands in his lap with palms upward, and eyes lowered. Those who listen to him preach, like the disciples of earlier hieratic art, sit with their palms together expressing reverence (see plates 3 and 11, pages 28 and 46).

In narrative art, including the engravings at Wat Si Chum, the reliefs at Wat Lai in Lopburi (see Fig. 5, page 130), the *Traibhumi* manuscript, and temple paintings, the various characters are found in many more active positions. Figures in the sculptures mentioned above may be seen flying, dancing, pointing, and shooting with bow and arrow. Those in paintings carry out the different actions described in the tales: lifting, swimming, climbing, leaping, reaching, running, and so on.

The postures are stylized and resemble frozen dance movements. Temiya, for example, tests his strength by using one arm to lift the chariot and one leg, on the same side of his body, to bear the weight. The other arm and leg are raised unnaturally high, as if he were about to leap (see Plate 4, page 33).

By exaggerating postures, the artist arrests the viewer's attention and draws his eye to the drama and significance of the event. The position in which Sakka may be found descending from the sky to end the sacrifice and save Canda-Kumara's life has its prototype in flying devas of Indian art. His legs are tucked up under him, while his upper half is engaged in reaching out. The upper half appears to float gracefully against the sky, while the tightly bent lower portion conveys the impression of speed and self-propulsion (see Plate 21, page 74).

This is a conceptual approach to the human figure in which the body is perceived as separate parts, in the same way that compositional elements are treated as segments. Each part of the body is shown from a different point of view. The king who shoots Sama, for example (see Plate 9, page 45), pulls back his bowstring in a way which defies nature. His face and lower legs are seen in profile, while his thighs, in a split position, are seen from the front. His upper body is seen from two points of view simultaneously. One side of the chest bulges out as if filled with air, while the other side appears concave as if seen in profile. A line extending from the top of the chest to the waist confirms that this is a front view of the chest.

The concave curve in the spine is characteristic of nearly all the postures of royalty and gods found in Thai painting, from the most quiet to the most active. Even commoners are found in clumsy postures that are variations of the above. Such a curve throws the shoulder and hip out of line. As such, it is not unlike the Indian S-shaped curve, called *tribhanga,* which pivots on the eyes, shoulders, and hips. In Thai art such a pose expresses static energy, whereas in Indian art it is meant to be more dynamic.

The painting style of Siam may have been influenced by the introduction of the shadow play into Thailand in the fifteenth century.[19] Thought to have originated in Java at a much earlier date, the shadow play is charazterized by exaggerated postures, faces in profile, flat puppets' bodies with flexible limbs and angular joints, and movements in only two directions, from side to side.[20] Many of the same features are seen in Thai dance dramas, which evolved in the seventeenth and eighteenth centuries.[21]

In Thai painting, as in Thai dance, emotions are expressed through gesture. Dance conventions do not permit emotions to be expressed on the dancer's face; as a result, feelings are revealed by a traditional pose or hand gesture, whether it be a tilt of the head, a twist of the fingers, a turn of the shoulder, or a swing of the hip. In both Thai painting and the dance, a lament, for example, is expressed by bending one arm gracefully upward and by tilting the hand and head toward each other. The opposite hand is usually held on the heart (see Plate 20, page 73). Arrogance is conveyed by planting one hand on a hip and brandishing the other (see Plate 25, page 87).

CONCLUSION In the evolution of Thai mural painting there is a shift from non-narrative subjects to narrative ones, bridged by manuscript painting and cloth banners, which include both. The traditional rows of Buddha figures, disciples, or thepchumnum evoke a tranquil atmosphere in a wat, conducive to meditation. The change to didactic themes reflects a growth in concern for the laity. The Jataka tales in particular provided a refreshing source of diversion and moral lessons for those whose religious interests needed stimulating.

Because Thai paintings stand at the far end of a tradition begun in India, continued in Ceylon, and cherished in Burma, one can trace various artistic elements to the conventions used in those countries. A synthesis of many influences, Siamese paintings can claim attention for their own elegant beauty and distinctive style. The delicately outlined, puppet-like figures, interacting before a fairy-tale landscape, exude a degree of energy and aplomb that lightens the heart.

Seen from afar, a mural is an abstract design of color and form, while the figures are minute and float against the surface. At close range the painting, like a puzzle, challenges the viewer to concentrate on each separate event and to fit the bits of the narrative together. An appropriate expression of the pragmatic outlook that Thai Buddhists have toward everyday life, Siamese pictorial art reflects the idea that every moment is fleeting and only the present one is real.

According to each viewer's understanding of the fragments, he will grasp the meaning of the Jataka tale and unify the composition in his own mind.

REFERENCE

LIST OF ALTERNATE SPELLINGS

CITIES

Phonetic	Graphic	Translation
Ayuthayā	Ayudhyā (Ayodhyā)	Ayodhyā, city of Rāma
Chonburī	Jalapurī	city of water
Lopburī	Lavapurī	city of Rāma's son
Nakhǫn Pathom	Nagara Paṭhama	first city
Nakhǫn Sī Thammarāt	Nagara Śrī Dharmarāja	city of the righteous king
Phetburī	Bejrapurī	diamond city
Sī Sachanālai	Śrī Sajjanālaya	place of good people
Sukhōthai	Sukhodaya	origin of happiness
Suphanburī	Suvarṇapurī	golden city
Thonburī	Dhanapurī	city of wealth

MONASTERIES

Wat Chūla Pathon	Cūḷa Padōṇa	the small padōṇa, in reference to the measuring cup used by the Brahmin Dōṇa to divide the Buddha's relics after his decease
Wat Machimāwāt	Majjhimāvāsa	middle-sized residence
Wat Mahāthāt	Mahādhātu	great relic; also a structure holding such a relic
Wat Phra Sī Sanphet	Śrī Sarbejña (Sarvajña)	the omniscient one
Wat Phra Thāt Lampang Luang	Braḥ Dhātu	holy reliquary
Wat Phumarinrāchapaksī	Bhumarindra-rājapakṣī	monastery of the queen bee
Wat Phuthaisawan	Buddhaiśvarya	kingdom of the Buddha
Wat Prāsāt	Prāsāda	royal building

Wat Rāchabūrana	Rājapūrana	perfected by the king
Wat Rāchasithārām	Rājasiddhārāma	monastery of the king's power
Wat Sī Chum	Śrī Jum	grove of bodhi trees
Wat Suwannārām	Suvarṇārāma	golden monastery
Wat Yai Inthārām	Indārāma	monastery of Indra's garden

NOTES

THE JATAKA TALES

1. T. W. Rhys Davids, *Buddhist Birth Stories* (London, 1880), p. xxxii.

2. Ibid., p. xxviii.

3. *The Ramayana and the Mahabharata*, condensed into English verse by Romesh C. Dutt (London, 1966), introductory note.

4. A. Foucher, *The Life of the Buddha*, abridged trans. by Simone B. Boas (Middletown, Conn., 1963), p. 242.

5. Christmas Humphreys, *Buddhism* (London, 1951), p. 45.

6. Ibid.

7. Gokuldas De, *The Significance and Importance of Jatakas* (Calcutta, 1951), p. xii.

8. Arya Sura, *Gatakamala*, trans. by J. S. Speyer, introd. by Max Müller (London, 1895), p. xv.

9. Rhys Davids, *Buddhist Birth Stories*, p. i.

10. Ibid., p. lvii.

11. Ibid., p. liv.

12. De, *Significance of Jatakas*, p. xv.

13. *Gatakamala*, p. xxv.

14. E. W. Adikaram, *Early History of Buddhism in Ceylon* (Colombo, 1946), p. 1.

15. Ibid., p. 2.

16. Rhys Davids, *Buddhist Birth Stories*, p. lvii.

17. Adikaram, *Buddhism in Ceylon*, p. 13.

18. V. Fausboll, *The Jataka Together with Its Commentary*, vol. 1 (London, 1897), p. 333.

19. G. Coedes, *The Indianized States of Southeast Asia* (Kuala Lumpur, 1968), p. 21.

20. A. Foucher, *The Beginnings of Buddhist Art*, trans. by L. A. Thomas and F. W. Thomas (Paris, 1917), pp. 52, 55–57.

21. De, *Significance of Jatakas*, p. 16.

22. Debala Mitra, *Sanchi* (New Delhi, 1965), pp. 27–29.

23. C. S. Sivaramamurti, *Amaravati Sculptures in the Madras Government Museum*, vol. 4 (Madras, 1942), pp. 207, 260–63.

24. Stella Kramrisch, *The Art of India* (London, 1955), pp. 200–201, plate p. 33.

25. P. R. Ramachandra Rao, *The Art of Nagarjunikonda* (Madras, 1956), p. 20.

26. Debala Mitra, *Ajanta* (New Delhi, 1968), p. 37.

27. Ibid., pp. 45, 51, 19.

28. Ibid., p. 27.

29. Nandadeva Wijesekera, *Early Sinhalese Painting* (Maharagama, Ceylon, 1959), p. 92.

30. Ibid.

31. Ibid., p. 47.

32. Ibid., p. 49.

33. Ibid., p. 47.

34. C. E. Godakumbura, *Murals at Tivanka Pilimage* (Colombo, 1969), p. 15.

35. C. E. Godakumbura, *Medawala Vihara Frescoes* (Colombo, n.d.), p. 13.

36. Mireille Bénisti, "Notes d'iconographie

khmère," *Bulletin de l'Ecole française d'Extrême-Orient*, vol. 51 (1963), p. 97.

37. Bruno Dagens, "Etude sur l'iconographie du Bayon (frontons et linteaux)," *Arts Asiatiques*, vol. 19 (1969), pp. 126, 129–30, 132–33, 135–36, 141–43.

38. Gordon H. Luce, "The 550 Jatakas in Old Burma," *Artibus Asiae*, vol. 19 (1969), p. 292.

39. Ibid.

40. Ibid.

41. Jane Gaston Mahler, "The Art of Medieval Burma in Pagan," *Archives of the Chinese Art Society of America*, vol. 41 (1958), p. 33.

42. Gordon H. Luce, *Old Burma–Early Pagan* (Locust Valley, N.Y., 1970), p. 44.

43. Ibid., p. 92.

44. Ibid., p. 47.

45. Ibid., p. 49.

46. Ibid., p. 47.

47. Luce, "The 550 Jatakas," p. 292.

48. Ibid., p. 295.

49. Luce, *Old Burma–Early Pagan*, p. 384.

50. A. B. Griswold, "Thoughts on a Centenary," *Journal of the Siam Society*, vol. 52, pt. 1 (April, 1964), p. 36.

51. A. B. Griswold, *Towards a History of Sukhodaya Art* (Bangkok, 1967), p. 3.

52. Ibid., p. 6.

53. Ibid., p. 7.

54. Ibid., p. 16.

55. Ibid., p. 30.

56. Ibid., p. 16.

57. Ibid., p. 42.

58. Ibid., p. 49.

59. Ibid., p. 17.

60. Ibid., p. 49.

61. Ibid., p. 41.

62. Ibid., p. 36.

63. A. B. Griswold and Prasert na Nagara, "The Inscription of Vat Traban Jan Phoak," *Journal of the Siam Society*, vol. 59, pt. 1 (January, 1971), p. 169.

64. Griswold, *Sukhodaya Art*, p. 55.

65. Ibid.

66. O. Frankfurter (trans.), "Events in Ayudhya from Chulasakaraj 686–966," *Journal of the Siam Society*, vol. 6, pt. 3 (1909), pp. 6–7.

67. Prince Dhani Nivat, *A History of Buddhism in Siam* (Bangkok, 1965), p. 9.

68. Silpa Bhirasri, *The Origin and Evolution of Thai Murals* (Bangkok, 1959), p. 33.

69. Ibid., p. 3.

70. Ibid., p. 6.

SIAMESE TEMPLE PAINTING

1. Bhirasri, *Thai Murals*, p. 13.

2. Ibid.

3. Ibid., p. 30.

4. Ibid., pp. 28–29.

5. Silpa Bhirasri, et al., *Murals of Nondburi School* (Bangkok, 1961), p. 16.

6. Jean Boisselier, "Les Peintures murales de Wat Ko Keo Suttharam (Phetburi)," *Felicitation Volumes of Southeast-Asian Studies*, vol. 2 (Bangkok, 1965), p. 339.

7. Silpa Bhirasri, *Thai Murals*, p. 32.

8. Ibid.

9. See Klaus Wenk, *Thailändische Miniaturmalerein* (Weisbaden, 1965).

10. A. B. Griswold and Prasert na Nagara, "The Inscription of Vat Jan Lom (1384 A.D.)," *Journal of the Siam Society*, vol. 59, pt. 1 (January, 1971), p. 204.

11. Ibid., p. 203.

12. Ibid.

13. Ibid., p. 204.

14. Elizabeth Lyons, "A Note on Thai Painting," *The Arts of Thailand* (Bloomington, 1960), p. 167.

15. Helen Duncan, "Acharn Lert Poung Pradej —A Master Artist," *Sawaddi* (May–June, 1967), p. 20.

16. Elizabeth Lyons, *Thai Traditional Painting* (Bangkok, 1963), p. 8.

17. Duncan, "Acharn Lert," p. 19.

18. Griswold, *Sukhodaya Art*, p. 5.

19. Prince Dhani Nivat, "The Shadow-Play as a Possible Origin of the Masked-Play," *Journal of the Siam Society* (November, 1969), p. 106.

20. Ibid., p. 109.

21. Ibid., p. 107.

GLOSSARY

Abhidamma Pitaka—texts on Buddhist metaphysics; the third part of the *Tipitaka,* the scriptures of Theravada Buddhism

Agni—Vedic god of fire

anga—classification in the oral canon of Theravada Buddhism, of which the Jataka is seventh

apsara—celestial dancer

arahat—an individual who achieves enlightenment through intense meditation

Aryan—belonging to the Caucasian race, one branch of which migrated into India from 1700 B.C. into the first millennium B.C., bringing a new culture and religion

asura—demon

atilavatthu—narrative portion of a Jataka tale in the fifth-century-A.D. *Jataka-Atthakatha;* contains original verse portions, or *gathas*

bai si—Thai name for ornamental vessel made of dried flowers or seashells, containing lustral water in its base; for use in wedding ceremonies

bhanakas—Buddhist monks who memorized and recited the Buddhist scriptures

Bodhi—Enlightenment; the name which has come to be associated with the pipal tree beneath which the Buddha achieved Enlightenment

Bodhisatta (Sanskrit: Bodhisattva)—in Pali, the language of Theravada Buddhism, the name given to a being who is destined to become a Buddha; in Mahayana Buddhism, has the additional meaning of one who has achieved Enlightenment but voluntarily postpones Nirvana in order to help all beings reach Nirvana

Bodhisattva—*see* Bodhisatta

bot (Pali: *uposatha;* Sanskrit: *upavasatha*)—abbreviated Thai name for *ubosot,* ordination hall of a Thai monastery

Brahma—Hindu god of creation; in Buddhist mythology, the chief god of the upper heavens

Brahma heavens—in Buddhist mythology, the sixteen heavens of form without sensory perception that are above the six lower heavens

Brahman—the universal spirit

Brahmanism—the religion of pre-Buddhist India that later evolved into Hinduism

Brahmin—a member of the priestly class of Hindus, who performs rituals on ceremonial occasions in both Buddhist and Hindu countries

Buddha—the Enlightened One

chedi (Pali: *cetiya;* Sanskrit: *chaitya*)—Thai name for stupa, originally a mound for relics of the Buddha; later considered a reminder of the Buddha whether it contained relics or not

cho fa—Thai term meaning "sky tassel"; the finial attached to the top corners of the roof of a Thai monastery building, usually the *bot* or *wihan*

Dasajati—Pali word for "Ten Births," referring to the last ten Jataka tales; see also *Thotsachat*

deva—a celestial being inhabiting of one of the six lower heavens of Buddhist cosmology; frequently seen in Thai mural painting in a worshiping posture

devi—feminine equivalent of *deva*

Dhamma (Sanskrit: Dharma)—Pali name for the doctrine of the Buddha

Dharani—name of the earth goddess; called Thorani in Thai

Dharma—*see* Dhamma

Dipavamsa—a fourth-century-A.D. Sinhalese chronicle

Dravidians—inhabitants of India before the arrival of the Aryans about 1700 B.C.

Dvaravati—name of the kingdom of the Mons in Thailand (sixth to tenth century A.D.); also its art style

Enlightenment—state of complete awareness and cognition of reality achieved by a Buddha; *see* Bodhi

fresco—in mural painting, the technique of applying paints to a layer of moist lime plaster

gandhabba (Sanskrit: *gandharva*)—celestial musician

garuda—mythical giant bird that can assume human form; in Hindu mythology, the mount of the god Vishnu

gathas—ancient verse of India; oldest part of the Jataka tales

ghee—clarified butter

Great Being—a Bodhisatta

Great Brahma—a Brahma who rules a Brahma heaven; *see* Brahma

hamsa—mythical goose or swan

Himavat—a mythical forest below the heavens of the gods and thought to be located in the Himalayas; inhabited by both imaginary and real animals

Hinayana—the "Lesser Vehicle" of Buddhism; another name for Theravada Buddhism, practiced in Ceylon, Burma, Thailand, Cambodia, and Laos

Hinduism—the prevailing religion of India today; primarily the worship of the gods Shiva and Vishnu

ho trai—the library of a Thai monastery, in which the *Tipitaka,* or Buddhist scriptures, are kept

Indra—Vedic god of thunder, called Sakka in Buddhist mythology; *see also* Sakka

jambu—rose apple

Jambudvipa—Indian name of the southern continent in Buddhist cosmology, where India is located

Jataka—birth story; usually considered tales of the previous lives of the Buddha

Jataka-Atthakatha—the Jataka tales and their commentaries; a fifth-century-A.D. compilation of Jataka tales comprising the Jataka verses and their commentaries. Only the verses are considered part of the Pali canon, the scriptures of Theravada Buddhism.

Kamma (Sanskrit: Karma)—Pali name for the law of cause and effect, which never ceases until the cycle of birth-death-rebirth ends in Nibbana

Karma—*see* Kamma

khamin—Thai name for turmeric, a yellow vegetable root used to test the receptiveness of a plaster wall surface before it is painted

Khmer—Cambodian empire of the eighth to fourteenth century A.D.

khoi paper—a type of soft cardboard used for Thai manuscripts after the fifteenth century

kinnari—female semidivine being whose upper half is human and lower half, bird; lives in the Himavat forest.

kinnara—masculine equivalent of *kinnari*

kranok—Thai name for the tripartite flame design representing the purifying flame of Buddhism

Kshatriya—member of the warrior class of India

kuti—Thai name for monks' living quarters at a monastery

Mahabharata—the great epic poem of India

Mahanipata—final division of the *Jataka-Atthakatha;* comprises the ten tales retold in this volume

Mahavamsa—a fifth-century-A.D. Sinhalese chronicle

Mahayana—the "Greater Vehicle," or northern school of Buddhism, practiced in Nepal, Tibet, China, Korea, and Japan

Manimekhala—goddess of lightning and guardian of seafarers

Mara—king of the forces of evil and temptation

Maurya—a powerful dynasty that ruled much of India in the third century B.C.

Meru—mythical mountain considered to be the core of the universe, on top of which is the abode of the gods; also called Sumeru and Sineru

Mon—early inhabitants of Thailand and one of the earliest peoples in Burma

mondop (Pali and Sanskrit: *mandapa*)—Thai name for a square monastery building used in Siam to hold a Buddha image or other reminder of the Buddha

naga—a mythical serpent that can assume human form at will

Nibbana (Sanskrit: Nirvana)—Pali term for the state of release from birth and death achieved by a Buddha

nikaya—a division of the *Suttanta-Pitaka,* part of the Pali canon, the scriptures of Theravada Buddhism

nipata—division of the *Jataka-Atthakatha,* the fifth-century-A.D. collection of Jataka tales

Nirvana—*see* Nibbana

paccupanna-vatthu—name of the introductory episode of a Jataka tale

Pali—a Prakrit dialect that became the canonical and liturgical language of Theravada Buddhism

peta (Sanskrit: *preta*)—ever-hungry ghost; from Buddhist mythology

Pitaka—basket; in Theravada Buddhism, one of the three major divisions of the scriptures; see *Tipitaka*

Prakrit—ancient spoken languages of India, related to Sanskrit

prang—a sanctuary tower crowned by several false stories

Pyu—early inhabitants of Burma, whose language belonged to the Tibeto-Burman group

Sakka—Buddhist name for the Vedic god of thunder, Indra; ruler of Tavatimsa heaven, abode of the thirty-three gods of Vedic origin

sala—community hall of a Thai monastery

samodhana—name of the conclusion of a Jataka tale

sangha—the Buddhist order of monks

Shiva—Hindu god of creation and destruction

sima stones—the stones around the ordination hall of a Theravadin monastery marking it as the property of the *sangha,* or order of monks

Sineru—another Pali name for Meru; *see* Meru

sing (Sanskrit: *sinha*)—Thai name for the mythical lion

Sinhalese—referring to Ceylon

stupa—see *chedi*

Sudra—member of the peasant class of India

Surya—Vedic god of the sun

Suttanta-Pitaka—discourses of the Buddha; one major division of the *Tipitaka,* the scriptures of Theravada Buddhism

Syam—original name for the Thai people

tamarind—a fruit whose seeds are roasted and made into a paste with chalk to smooth a wall surface before it can be painted in Thai tempera technique

tapas—burning glow; state of spiritual bliss

Tavatimsa heaven—the heaven of the thirty-three gods whose king is Sakka; second lowest of the six heavens of form and sensory perception

tempera—in Thailand, the technique of applying paints mixed with gum or glue to a dry, desalinated plaster wall surface

thepchumnum—Thai name for rows of devas, garudas, and yakkhas in positions of reverence, painted on the walls of a Thai *bot* or *wihan*

Theravada—literally, "Doctrine of the Elders," another name for Hinayana Buddhism; *see also* Hinayana

Tipitaka (Sanskrit: *Tripitaka*)—literally, "Three Baskets"; the name of the Pali canon, or scriptures of Theravada Buddhism

Thotsachat—Thai name for the last ten Jatakas; see also *Dasajati*

torana—carved gates in the stone fence surrounding an Indian stupa

Traibhumi—the Three Worlds of Buddhist cosmology; also the name of a treatise written by the Thai king Lu Thai in 1340; also the name of Thai manuscripts illustrating the Three Worlds

tribhanga—an S-shaped pose pivoting on the eyes, shoulders, and hips; part of the Indian canon of painting

Tripitaka—see *Tipitaka*

ubosot—see *bot*

Vaisya—member of the merchant class of India

Vedic—concerning the Vedas, the religious texts of the Aryan peoples who migrated to India from 1700 B.C. into the first millennium

veyyakarana—name of the commentary section of a Jataka tale

Vinaya-Pitaka—text of the disciplines of the monastic order; part of the *Tipitaka,* the scriptures of Theravada Buddhism

Vishnu—Hindu god; the preserver

Vissakamma (Sanskrit: Visvakarma)—Hindu god of architecture

wai—a gesture of respect and greeting that originated in India and is used widely in Thailand; placing the palms of the hands together, then bringing the tips of the fingers to the nose and bowing the head at the same time

wai khru—the Thai ceremony of paying respect to teachers

wat—Thai monastery complex

wihan (Pali and Sanskrit: *vihara*)—Thai name for the assembly and worship hall of a Buddhist monastery

withayathon (Sanskrit: *vidyadhara*)—Thai name for a hermit, who may be depicted flying in the clouds as a result of intense meditation or magical powers

yakkha (Sanskrit: *yaksha*)—originally a tree spirit and guardian of the hidden wealth of the world; subject to Kubera, god of wealth; sometimes a demon with superhuman powers

BIBLIOGRAPHY

Adikaram, E. W. *Early History of Buddhism in Ceylon*. Colombo, 1946

Aggamahapandita, A. P., Buddhadatta Mahathera, ed. *Jinakalamali*. Transcribed from a Siamese text. London, 1962

Alabaster, Henry. *The Wheel of the Law*. London, 1871

Annual Report, 1930–34, pt. 2. Archaeological Survey of India, Delhi, 1963

Archer, W. G. *Indian Miniatures*. London, 1960

Arya Sura. *Gatakamala, or Garland of Birth Stories*. Trans. by J. S. Speyer. London, 1895

Auboyer, Jeannine. *Daily Life in Ancient India*. London, 1961

———, and Goepper, Roger. *The Oriental World*. New York, 1967

Ba Shin, Bohmu. *The Lokahteikpan: Early Burmese Culture in a Pagan Temple*. Rangoon, 1962

Bailey, Dorothy. "The Glories of Wisdom—Mahosadha in Murals." *Sawaddi*, September–October, 1969, pp. 7–9

———. "The Greatest Sage." *Sawaddi*, September–October, 1969, pp. 4–6

Basham, A. L. *The Wonder That Was India*. New York, 1954

Bénisti, Mireille. "Notes d'iconographie khmère." *Bulletin de l'Ecole française d'Extrême-Orient*, vol. 51 (1963), pp. 95–98

Bhirasri, Silpa. *Appreciation of Our Murals*. Bangkok, 1959

———. *The Origin and Evolution of Thai Murals*. Bangkok, 1959

———. *Thai Buddhist Art*. Bangkok, 1963

———. *Thai Buddhist Sculpture*. Bangkok, 1946

Bhirasri, Silpa; Haribhitak, Fua; and Yimsiri, Khien. *Murals of Nondburi School*. Bangkok, 1961

Boisselier, Jean. "Les peintures murales de Wat Ko Keo Suttharam (Phetburi)." *Felicitation Volumes of Southeast-Asian Studies*, vol. 2. Bangkok, 1965

Bowie, Theodore, ed. *The Arts of Thailand*. Bloomington, 1960

———. *East–West in Art*. Bloomington, 1966

Buddhadasa, Bhikku. *Teaching Dhamma by Pictures*. Bangkok, 1969

Buribhand, Luang Boribal, and Griswold, A. B. *The Royal Monasteries and Their Significance*. Bangkok, 1968

Campbell, Joseph. *The Masks of God: Oriental Mythology*. New York, 1962

Coedes, G. *Angkor*. London, 1963

———. *The Indianized States of Southeast Asia*. Ed. by Walter F. Vella; trans. by Susan Brown Cowing. Kuala Lumpur, 1968

Conze, Edward. *Buddhism: Its Essence and Development*. New York, 1959

Coomaraswamy, Ananda K. *The Aims of Indian Art*. Broad Campden, England, 1908

———. *Medieval Sinhalese Art*. New York, 1956

Cowell, E. B., and Rouse, W. H. D., trans. *The Jataka, or Stories of the Buddha's Former Births.* Cambridge, 1907

Dagens, Bruno. "Etude sur l'iconographie du Bayon (frontons et linteaux)." *Arts Asiatiques,* vol. 19 (1969), pp. 123–67

Damrong Rajanubhab, Prince. *A History of Buddhist Monuments in Siam.* Bangkok, 1962

De, Gokuldas. *The Significance and Importance of Jatakas.* Calcutta, 1951

Dhanapala, D. B. *The Story of Sinhalese Painting.* Maharayama, Ceylon, 1957

Dhani Nivat, Prince. *Collected Articles. Journal of the Siam Society,* Bangkok, 1969

———. *A History of Buddhism in Siam.* Bangkok, 1965

———. *The Royal Palaces.* Bangkok, 1968

Duncan, Helen. "Acharn Lert Poung Pradej—A Master Artist." *Sawaddi,* May–June, 1967, pp. 4–5, 19–22

Dutt, Romesh C. *The Ramayana and the Mahabharata.* London, 1966

Eliot, Charles. *Hinduism and Buddhism: An Historical Sketch,* vols. 2 and 3. London, 1921

Fausboll, V. *The Jataka Together with Its Commentary,* vol. 1. London, 1897

Feer, M. L. *A Study of the Jatakas.* Calcutta, 1963 (original edition 1875)

Feroci, C. (Silpa Bhirasri). "Traditional Thai Painting." In *Selected Articles from the Siam Society Journal: 1929–1953,* vol. 2, pp. 280–88. Bangkok, 1954

Foucher, A. *The Beginnings of Buddhist Art.* Trans. by L. A. Thomas and F. W. Thomas. Paris, 1917

———. *The Life of the Buddha.* Abridged trans. by Simone B. Boas. Middletown, Conn., 1963

Fournereau, Lucien. *Le Siam ancien.* 2 vols. Paris, 1895, 1908

Frankfurter, O., trans. "Events in Ayuddhya from Chulasakaraj 686–966." *Journal of the Siam Society,* vol. 6, pt. 3 (1909), pp. 3–21

Frazer, James G. *The Golden Bough.* New York, 1940

Frederic, Louis. *The Art of India: Temples and Sculpture.* New York, n.d.

———. *The Temples and Sculpture of Southeast Asia.* London, 1965

Gedney, William J. Review of *From Ancient Thai to Modern Dialects,* by J. Marvin Brown. *Social Science Review,* vol. 3, no. 2 (September, 1965), pp. 107–12

Ghosh, A., ed. *Ajanta Murals.* New Delhi, 1967

Godakumbura, C. E. *Medawala Vihara Frescoes.* Colombo, n.d.

———. *Murals at Tivanka Pilimage.* Colombo, 1969

Goonsekere, I. A. *Buddhist Commentarial Literature.* Kandy, Ceylon, 1967

Griswold, Alexander B. "The Architecture and Sculpture of Siam." In *The Arts of Thailand,* ed. by Theodore Bowie, pp. 25–165. Bloomington, 1960

———. *Dated Buddha Images of Northern Siam.* Ascona, Switzerland, 1957

———. *King Mongkut of Siam.* New York, 1961

———. "Thoughts on a Centenary." *Journal of the Siam Society,* vol. 52, pt. 1 (April, 1964), pp. 21–55

———. *Towards a History of Sukhodaya Art.* Bangkok, 1967

———; Kim, Chewon; and Pott, Peter H. *Burma, Korea, Tibet.* London, 1964

Griswold, A. B., and Na Nagara, Prasert. "The Inscription of Vat Traban Jan Phoak (Face I, 1380 A.D.; Face II, 14th century, date uncertain): Epigraphic and Historical Studies No. 7." *Journal of the Siam Society,* vol. 59, pt. 1 (January, 1971), pp. 157–88

———. "The Inscription of Vat Jan Lom (1384 A.D.): Epigraphic and Historical Studies No. 8." *Journal of the Siam Society,* vol. 59, pt. 1 (January, 1971), pp. 189–208

Groslier, Bernard. *Indochina.* London, 1962

Hall, D. G. E. *A History of Southeast Asia.* London, 1954

Hardy, R. Spence. *A Manual of Buddhism.* Calcutta, 1967 (original edition 1853)

Hastings, James, ed. *Encyclopedia of Religion and Ethics.* New York, 1961

Holt, Claire. *The Art of Indonesia.* Ithaca, N.Y., 1967

Humphreys, Christmas. *Buddhism*. London, 1951

Ions, Veronica. *Indian Mythology*. London, 1967

Isherwood, Christopher, and Prabhavananda, Swami. *Bhagavad Gita: The Song of God*. London, 1947

Kempers, A. J. Bernet. *Ancient Indonesian Art*. Cambridge, Mass., 1959

Kennedy, Victor. "The Rise and Decline of Thai Mural Painting." *Bangkok Post Sunday Magazine*, March 24, 1968

Khantipalo, Bhikku. *Buddhism Explained*. Bangkok, 1968

Khokasanthiya, Mali. *Guide to Old Sukhothai*. Trans. by Hiram W. Woodward, Jr. Bangkok, 1971

Kramrisch, Stella. *The Art of India*. London, 1955

Le May, Reginald. *Buddhist Art in Siam*. London, 1938

———. *The Culture of Southeast Asia*. London, 1954

Lee, Sherman E. *A History of Far Eastern Art*. New York, 1965

Life of the Buddha According to Thai Temple Paintings. U.S. Information Service, Bangkok, 1957

Lu Pe Win, U. *Pictorial Guide to Pagan*. Rangoon, 1963

Luce, Gordon H. "The 550 Jatakas in Old Burma." *Artibus Asiae*, vol. 19 (1969), pp. 291–307

———. *Old Burma–Early Pagan*. Locust Valley, N.Y., 1970

———, and Ba Shin, Bohmu. "A Chieng Mai Mahathera Visits Pagan (1393 A.D.)." *Artibus Asiae*, vol. 24, pp. 330–37

Lyons, Elizabeth. "Arts of the Bangkok Period." In *Silpa Samaya U Dong*. Bangkok, 1967

———. "A Note on Thai Painting." In *The Arts of Thailand*, ed. by Theodore Bowie. Bloomington, 1960, pp. 166–81

———. *Thai Traditional Painting*. Bangkok, 1963

———. *The Tosachat in Thai Painting*. Bangkok, 1963

Mahler, Jane Gaston. "The Art of Medieval Burma in Pagan." *Archives of the Chinese Art Society of America*, vol. 41 (1958), pp. 30–47

Martini, Ginette. "Les titres des Jataka dans les manuscrits pali de la Bibliothèque Nationale de Paris." *Bulletin de l'Ecole française d'Extrême-Orient*, vol. 51 (1963), pp. 79–93

Mitra, Debala. *Ajanta*. New Delhi, 1968

———. *Sanchi*. New Delhi, 1965

Mote, Frederick. "Problems of Thai Prehistory." *Social Science Review*, vol. 2, pt. 2 (October, 1964), pp. 100–109

Müller, Max. Introduction to *Gatakamala, or Garland of Birth Stories*, by Arya Sura, trans. by J. S. Speyer. London, 1895

Musaeus-Higgins, Marie. *Jatakamala, or a Garland of Birth Stories*. Colombo, 1914

Pan Hla, Nai. "Mon Literature and Culture." *Journal of the Burma Royal Society*, vol. 41, pp. 65–75

Pande, Govind Chandra. *Studies in the Origins of Buddhism*. Allahabad, 1957

Quaritch Wales, H. G. *Dvaravati*. London, 1969

———. *Siamese State Ceremonies*. London, 1931

Rahula, Walpole. *History of Buddhism in Ceylon*. Colombo, 1956

Rajadhon, Phya Anuman. *Essays on Thai Folklore*. Bangkok, 1968

Rao, P. R. Ramachandra. *The Art of Nagarjunikonda*. Madras, 1956

Rapson, E. G., ed. *Cambridge History of India*. London, 1922

Rawson, Philip. *The Art of Southeast Asia*. New York, 1967

Ray, Nihar-Rangan. *Brahmanical Gods of Burma*. Calcutta, 1932

Rhys Davids, Caroline Augusta. *Sakya, or Buddhist Origins*. London, 1931

Rhys Davids, T. W. *Buddhist Birth Stories*. London, 1880

———. *Buddhist India*. Calcutta, 1903

Rosenfield, Clare S. "Birds of a Feather." *Sawaddi*, March–April, 1970, pp. 4–7

———. "The Mythical Animal Statues at the Prasat Phrathepphabidon." In *In Memoriam Phya Anuman Rajadhon*, ed. by Tej Bunnag and Michael Smithies. Bangkok, 1970, pp. 273–300

Ross, Nancy Wilson. *Three Ways of Asian Wisdom*. New York, 1966

Rowland, Benjamin. *Ajanta*. New York, 1963

————. *The Art and Architecture of India: Buddhist, Hindu, Jain*. Baltimore, 1953

————. *Art in East and West*. Boston, 1964

————. *The Evolution of the Buddha Image*. New York, 1963

————. *The Wall-Paintings of India, Central Asia, and Ceylon*. Boston, 1938

Seckel, Dietrich. *The Art of Buddhism*. London, 1964

Siddiqui, S. *A Pictorial Guide to Aurangabad, Daulatabad, Ellora and Ajanta*. Aurangabad, 1969

Sivaramamurti, C. S. *Amaravati Sculptures in the Madras Government Museum*. Madras, 1942

Smith, V. A. *Early History of India*. Oxford, 1908

Spratt, Manaktalas. *Hindu Culture and Personality: A Psychoanalytic Study*. Bombay, 1966

Sukhosophy, Thepsiri. "Wichanphonngan nai Chadok." *Withayasanparithat*, January 5, 1970, pp. 33–34

Swaan, Wim. *Lost Cities of Asia: Ceylon, Pagan, Angkor*. New York, 1966

Traibhumi manuscripts, ca. 1550 and 1776. Bangkok, National Library

Vella, Walter F. *Siam Under Rama III*. New York, 1957

Wagner, Frits A. *Indonesia*. Trans. by Ann E. Keep. London, 1959

Wenk, Klaus. *Thailändische Miniaturmalerein*. Weisbaden, 1965

Wheatley, P. *The Golden Khersonese*. Kuala Lumpur, 1961

Wijesekera, Nandadeva. *Ancient Painting and Sculpture in Ceylon*. Colombo, 1962

————. *Early Sinhalese Painting*. Maharagama, Ceylon, 1959

Winstedt, Richard, ed. *Indian Art*. London, 1966

Yimsiri, Khien. "The Evolution of Traditional Thai Painting." In *The Evolution of Certain Aspects of Thai Art*. Unpublished

Zimmer, Heinrich. *The Art of Indian Asia*. New York, 1955

————. *Myths and Symbols in Indian Art and Civilization*. New York, 1946

ABOUT THE AUTHORS

Elizabeth Wray, a graduate of Vassar and a teacher by profession, lived in Bangkok for seven years, and was the chief organizer of the National Museum Work Study Group formed in 1968, an active force in popularizing Thai art and culture. Clare Rosenfield, educated at Smith College and Columbia University, and Dorothy Bailey, a graduate of the University of Massachusetts, both lived in Thailand for many years and wrote on Thai and Indian art and mythology. Elizabeth Wray's husband, pediatrician Joe D. Wray, served as the book's photographer and illustrator.

The "weathermark" identifies this book as a production of Weatherhill, Inc., publishers of fine books on Asia and the Pacific. Book design and typography: Meredith Weatherby. Cover design: Mariana Canelo. Printing and binding: Oceanic Graphics Printing, Hong Kong.